Singing to Liberation

*Songs of Freedom
and Nights of Resistance
on Indian Campuses*

Suddhabrata Deb Roy

Daraja Press

Published by
Daraja Press
https://darajapress.com
Wakefield, Québec, Canada

© 2023 Suddhabrata Deb Roy
All rights reserved

ISBN: 9781990263491

Cover design: Kate McDonell

Library and Archives Canada Cataloguing in Publication

Title: Singing to liberation : songs of resistance and nights of liberation on Indian campuses / Suddhabrata Deb Roy ; foreword by Taimur Rehman, Laal, Pakistan ; afterword by Ndindi Kitonga, PALMS, US.
Names: Deb Roy, Suddhabrata, 1993- author.
Description: Includes bibliographical references.
Identifiers: Canadiana 20230530877 | ISBN 9781990263491 (softcover)
Subjects: LCSH: Social change—India. | LCSH: Protest movements—India. | LCSH: Politics and culture— India. | LCSH: Protest songs—India. | LCSH: College campuses—India.
Classification: LCC HM831 .D39 2023 | DDC 303.48/40954—dc23

For the cultural activists out there
who have kept on singing songs of liberation and emancipation
during these dark days.
Thank You!

दीप जिसका महल्लात ही में जले
चंद लोगों की ख़ुशियों को लेकर चले
वो जो साए में हर मसलहत के पले
ऐसे दस्तूर को सुब्हे बेनूर को
मैं नहीं मानता, मैं नहीं जानता |
मैं भी ख़ाइफ़ नहीं तख़्ता-ए-दार से
मैं भी मंसूर हूँ कह दो अग़्यार से
क्यूँ डराते हो ज़िंदाँ की दीवार से
ज़ुल्म की बात को जहल की रात को
मैं नहीं मानता मैं नहीं जानता |

— Habib Jalib (1928-1993), Revolutionary Poet

[The light that shines only in palaces,
Burns up the joy of the people in the shadows,
Derives its strength from others' weakness
That kind of system, like dawn without light,
I refuse to acknowledge, I refuse to accept!
I am not afraid of execution,
Tell the world that I am a martyr
How can you frighten me with prison walls?
This overhanging doom, this night of ignorance,
I refuse to acknowledge,
I refuse to accept!]

Contents

Preface and Acknowledgements — i

Foreword: Singing For the Revolution: A Laal Journey — *Taimur Rahman* — iii

Introduction: Culture as Resistance, Culture as Dissent! — 1

1 The Transcending Nature of Cultural Protests — 17

2 Students' Rebellions and the Cultural Movement — 32

3 The Questioning of Modernity — 45

4 Dangers of Cultural Resistance under Hindutva — 55

5 Cultural Struggles and the Contradictions of India — 65

6 Articulating Everyday Contradictions — 82

7 Cultural Resistance and Revolutionary Subjectivity — 92

Conclusion: Can one Sing to Liberation in 'Unreal' Spaces'? — 103

Afterword: Yes, to our Songs of Liberation! Yes, to Freedom! — *Ndindi Kitonga* — 119

Preface and Acknowledgements

This book was both a planned and an unplanned venture. It was planned in the way that I did hope to write something of this kind, but probably a lot later. It was unplanned in the way that by the time I got down to actually thinking about it, I realized that I had already drafted most of the things which were supposed to be in the book. This book, I must admit, is not a scholarly outburst but rather a reflection of my own experiences and my own inferences based on them. This book, in other words, is a result of my decade-long experience with and within the students' movement in India. In many ways, as a generation, those of us – who have just begun to be in our 30s and continue to feel like we are in our 20s, are a historic generation because our beginning of studentships mostly coincided with the rise of the Hindutva regime in India.

This book, more than anybody else owes itself to my parents, who supported me – both financially and ideologically.

Marcelle Dawson, my Doctoral Supervisor, for being a pillar of support. Annabel Cooper and Simon Barber, my co-supervisors, for standing by me.

Kevin Anderson, Peter Hudis, Sandra Rein, Grace, Kieran and Jonas, who have constantly been my greatest support systems, as well as my harshest critics.

Rebecca Stringer, conversations, and discussions with whom has really enriched me.

Thanks to Debasreeta for standing with me.

Comrades in Assam who have been instrumental to this journey. I will not name anybody because of the perennial risk associated with my dodgy memory as far as names are concerned.

Friends, Comrades and Foes at the Hyderabad Central University in India, without whose help, criticism, and support this would have been impossible.

Friends and Comrades at the University of Otago who continue to support me, especially Brandon, Angus, and Natasha. Friends and Comrades across different student organizations such as the Students' Federation of India (SFI), the All India Students' Association (AISA), the All India Students' Federation (AISF), the Ambedkar Students' Association (ASA), the Dalit Students' Union (DSU), the Muslim Students' Federation (MSF), the All India Democratic Students' Organisation (AIDSO), the Tribal Students' Forum (TSF), the Birsa Ambedkar Phule Students Association (BAPSA), the All Assam Muslim Students' Union (AAMSU), the Students Islamic Organisation (SIO), and others. Conversations with you that I have had over the years are really the soul of the book.

Comrades at the International Marxist-Humanist Organisation (IMHO) for supporting me in my endeavors and for providing me with a safe space to discuss my ideas.

I would like to thank Dr Taimur Rahman for the excellent foreword that he has written for the work. It was in 2012, that somebody introduced me to the music of Laal, and I have been a passionate fanboy since then. It is indeed a great honor for me to have a foreword written by him. His lectures on YouTube regarding philosophy and politics are something that I would recommend to anyone looking for simple explanations of difficult terms.

Thanks to Dr Ndindi Kitonga, a longtime friend and fellow traveller in the journey to ensuring social justice, for penning down the beautiful afterword for the book. Ndindi is one of the most dedicated activists I have known in my short life, and her strength and courage have always been a source of deep inspiration for me.

Most importantly, this book would not have seen the light of day without the help from Firoze Manji of Daraja Press, who continues to support me and others like me from the Global South to make our voices heard.

Foreword
Singing For the Revolution: A Laal Journey

Taimur Rahman

Associate Professor, Lahore University of Management Sciences, Lead Guitarist and Spokesperson of the Marxist Band 'Laal', Secretary-General of the Mazdoor Kisan Party (MKP), Pakistan

In 2006 Pakistani lawyers erupted in protest against the military dictatorship of General Pervez Musharraf. This movement was dubbed the Lawyers Movement by the media. However, there was one aspect of this movement that was somewhat uncharacteristic of the stereotype of social movements in Pakistan. It was accompanied by a soundtrack by a band called Laal (which means red). Explicit in their communist views, the band was nonetheless thrust into the limelight by an otherwise conservative media. Thanks to GEO TV, their album Umeed e Sahar became almost synonymous with the movement. Their music videos were playing almost 20 times a day on what was then Pakistan's most-watched news channel. Thus, Pakistan got to see the strange phenomenon of a communist band playing rock music on a capitalist television channel for a middle-class movement. Those heady days were over a decade ago. In between working on my PhD, organizing protests, and ensuring my wife and I were living within the means of our scholarship, we were writing songs of protests inspired by Bob Marley, Tracy Chapman, Nusrat & Pathanay Khan. But like all heady days, they were, or, at least felt, far too short.

The dictatorship was removed, elections were held, business at its apathetic usual returned to Pakistan. Except, this is

Pakistan, and business as usual is always an unexplainable mix of apathy and medieval authoritarian barbarity. From 2007, a new medieval movement called Tehreek e Taliban Pakistan had declared war on the state and society of Pakistan. Their terrorist attacks were not confined just to the state but included schools, hospitals, airports, parks, and markets. Thousand were blown from limb to limb in a grotesque macabre campaign of death and destruction. Worst of all, public opinion polls indicated, despite all the evidence of death and destruction, that a substantial body of young people even empathized with some version of this. rough shariah justice. This, of course, was referred to as the "Zia generation"; young people who had grown up and been educated either during the period of Zia ul Haq's draconian martial law or educated in the ideological system set up to support his process of "Islamisation".

What could be done? Political parties were too afraid to speak up. The state was hesitant to act decisively. The media was reporting the violent attacks but was careful not to take a side. Pakistani society did not cower under military dictatorship but seemed to have cowered under the combination of religion and violence. At first, we began to make songs against extremism. But no one would play them. And even social media didn't have any substantive appetite for such a blatantly and openly anti-extremist message. That is when we began to develop the campaign that is now called "Music for Peace", a campaign to recall tolerant and open-minded outlooks of the folk tradition before this barbaric extremism. If the people wouldn't come to us, we had to go to the people.

So Laal hit the road. We started visiting small towns, villages, urban slums, colleges, schools, and universities. Pretty much any place where we could get a few people to sit down and listen. Without any substantive support at any level, all of this was at first haphazard, disorganized, unplanned, and even a bit random. We didn't even have the right equipment for such a grassroots campaign. The one thing we did not lack was enthusiasm. Just a kind of stupidity, ignorance, an arrogant but youthful disregard for received and accepted wisdom. Little by little we gained momentum, experience, organization, and understanding. A decade later, we have lost track, but a rough estimate is that Laal performed over 600 grassroots concerts all over Pakistan. Before the BJP government came to power, Laal would also visit India at least a few times every year. Perhaps our most memorable concert was the one held at the Jawaharlal Nehru University, where an audience of thousands joined us in song and slogans. The atmosphere of friendship between Pakistan and India resonated through the stony red bricks of that historic and hallowed institution. It would be difficult to capture in mere words the experiences of this campaign, the joy of seeing young faces beaming with excitement and joy, the sense of community and togetherness as people sing together. The myth of a people so bamboozled by religion that they could not appreciate poetry, music, and performing arts lay shattered before our feet. And the myth that the people were too ground down by poverty to appreciate art and literature proved to be nothing but an elitist prejudice. We sang, we laughed, we danced, we joked with the people. We felt the walls of class, caste, privilege and hatred crumble in those moments of ecstasy.

Will we live to see the day when these moments turn into more than mere moments? Will there be a time when we arrive at our destination? On the other hand, is arriving really so important? Perhaps it is the journey and not arriving that is the very essence of life. Every exhausting journey of hundreds of miles to far-away communities ends the same way. With all of us making the return journey covered from head to toe in sweat but with a sense of having taken yet another small step towards that tomorrow where not merely communities, but the world will sing together. That may sound terribly idealistic. And it is. But what is a life without ideals, without a noble end, without dreams? As John Lennon put it so succinctly:

> *You may say I'm a dreamer*
> *but I'm not the only one.*
> *I hope someday you'll join us,*
> *and the world will live as one.*

If "singing for [or to] the revolution" is the slogan of this book, Laal has lived its reality.

Introduction
Culture as Resistance, Culture as Dissent!

> Culture is the whole way of life,
> of a given human community.
> Faiz Ahmed Faiz[1]

India underwent a process of rapid socio-political and cultural transformation in 2014 when the Bhartiya Janta Party came to power in New Delhi under the leadership of Narendra Modi. The effects of the transformation got further consolidated in 2019 when Narendra Modi was re-elected as the Prime Minister of the largest democracy in the world – with a record-breaking margin for the BJP. The rampant rise of the far-right in India led by the Rashtriya Swayamsevak Sangh (RSS) and its political front, the BJP led by Narendra Modi have launched an attack on the very soul of India. They have caused an erosion of the secular and democratic ethos of the Indian society, which it had maintained albeit with its own set of contradictions since 1947. The Narendra Modi-led Central Government in India has been known for its hostile attitude towards Muslims, Dalits, women and in general against those who dissent against it, mainly the students. The neo-fascist nature of the BJP has been highlighted not only through the material violence that it has unleashed on the marginalized sections of the populace but also through its constant attempts at controlling the cultural discourse of the

---

[1] Faiz, F. A. 'Problems of Cultural Planning in Asia—With Special Reference to Pakistan'. In S. Majeed (ed), *Culture and Identity: Selected English Writings of Faiz*. Oxford: Oxford University Press, 2005.

country. In its drive to bring into effect a majoritarian Hindutva-centric nation-state, the BJP has been on a rampage curtailing the freedom of speech and cultural expression of the people. The desired control over the cultural fabric of society has been brought into effect through massive policing of civil society, domination over the public discourse and absolute control over the mainstream media and cultural forms of expression, which have left an indelible mark on not only the political fabric of India but also on its cultural fabric.

The cultural fabric of the society plays an important role in the way in which a society addresses the contradictions that exist in the society because it is critical to the development of the ways in which human beings interpret their social existence and the ways in which they can potentially hope to transform it. It is, in other words, a whole way of life itself.[2] Culture and the mediums associated with it as such have always played an important role in revolutions across the globe.[3] They have often resulted in a new form of cultural expression that has been able to develop a new form of hegemony in the society,[4] while at times they have also resulted in a new way of interpreting the society around oneself.[5] Culture, as Raymond Williams argues, is a way of interpreting the whole history and sociology of a particular civilization itself giving rise to very specific ideas and social practices,[6] which often

---

[2] Eagleton, T. *Culture*. London: Yale University Press, 2016.

[3] Mally, L. *Culture of the Future: The Proletkult Movement in Revolutionary Russia*. Berkeley: The University of California Press, 1990; Szemere, A. 'Bandits, Heroes, the Honest, and the Misled: Exploring the Politics of Representation in the Hungarian Uprising of 1956'. In L. Grossberg, C. Nelson, & P. Treichler (eds), *Cultural Studies*. New York: Routledge, 1992; Adhikari, A. *The Bullet and the Ballot Box: The Story of Nepal's Maoist Revolution*. London: Verso, 2014.

[4] Zhang, L. *Red Legacies in China: Cultural Afterlives of the Communist Revolution*. Harvard University Press, 2016; Chetna, N. M. *Three Decades of Dandakaranya Literary and Cultural Movement 1980-2010: People's War is the Refrain of the Song*. Kolkata: SETU, 2017.

[5] Mercer, K. '"1968": Periodizing Postmodern Politics and History'. In L. Grossberg, C. Nelson, & P. Treichler (eds), *Cultural Studies*. New York: Routledge, 1992.

[6] Williams, R. *Marxism and Literature*. Oxford: Oxford University Press, 1977; Williams, R. *Culture and Materialism*. London: Verso, 1980.

become the basis of the contradictions that dominate contemporary human life.[7] Culture can be understood in two distinct ways, first as a culture with a small c that refers to a set of societal values and norms often in an anthropological sense. Culture can also be understood as Culture with a Capital C, which denotes culture as a tangible entity, an artifact imagined by an artist or a practitioner of culture.[8]

Civilizations across the globe have been based out of certain cultural traits, but to become a civilization per se, only the possession of culture is often never sufficient but rather requires an ambition to develop and grow, and a material force which can make it happen.[9] It is the dialectical relationship between these two aspects that produces the contours within which a significant section of the marginalized population frames their social existence, especially with regard to the movements against social injustice that they participate in. The analysis of culture and cultural artifacts becomes critical because the world today is constructed by a myriad of signs and symbols that influence human ontology and the epistemology that they produce.[10] Cultural values have an intrinsic connection with issues such as social marginality, status, and socio-economic stability. The question of culture is a central one in the context of India because of the complexities that the Indian society has come to harbour since centuries of existence. Cultural factors can promote or restrict social mobility within the conditions that India presents,[11] as many activists will highlight in this book. It is this innate ability of cultural resistance that has made it so attractive to the student movement. Take the following lines from a poem:

---

[7] Marcuse, H. *Eros and Civilization*. London: ARK, 1952.

[8] Hall, S. 'Culture, the Media and the "Ideological Effect"'. In J Curran, M. Gurevitch, & J., Woolacott (eds.), *Mass Communication and Society*. New York: Edward Arnold, 1977.

[9] Debray, R. 'Civilization, a Grammar: Imprint, Impress, Imperium'. *New Left Review*, 2(107), 2017, 33-44.

[10] Perry, N. *The Dominion of Signs*. Auckland: Auckland University Press, 1994.

[11] Desai, A. R. 'Sociological Problems of Economic Development'. In A. R. Desai (ed), *Rural Sociology in India*. Bombay: Popular Prakashan, 1969.

कथा सुनो रे लोगो, एक कथा सुनो रे लोगो,
हैं हम मजदूर की करुण कहानी और करीब से जानो [...]
अपनी मेहनत से भाई, धरती कू हुई खुदाई, माटी ने बीज को बोया, धरती को दुल्हन बनाई
पसीना हमने ही बहाया, भूपति ने खूब काम्या, सौकर के सूद ने हमको, सौकर के कर्ज ने हमको
गाओ से शहर में भाग्य, अरे दाने दाने को साथ जोड़कर जीने की कठिनाई, ऐसा क्यों है भाई?
क्युकी?
ये सामंती राज हैं,
खाने को खाना नहीं, पीने को पानी नहीं,
रहने को घर नहीं, पहनने को कपडा नहीं,
ये कैसा राज है भाई! ये झूठा राज है भाई![12]

[Listen to a story, Listen to a story, This is the story of an exploited worker which you can know very intimately, [...] We have harvested the land with our sweat, Through our hard work we have transformed the barren land into a beautiful bride, But it is the feudal lord who earned the money, and we poor workers got further exploited when the moneylender made us pay high interests; Our loans pushed us to the cities, where we faced further purges of hunger. Why is it like this? Because this is a Feudal Rule, where we do not have food to eat, Water to drink, Homes to live in, Clothes to wear; What kind of Rule is this? This is a Misrule!][13]

While the above lines are more analytical in nature reflecting upon the state of the working class in India, one can take a more direct action-centred poem as another example:

---

[12] Lyrics available from https://poetly-substack-com.translate.goog/p/katha-suno-re-logo-as-featured-in?_x_tr_sl=en&_x_tr_tl=hi&_x_tr_hl=hi&_x_tr_pto=tc,sc [Accessed 26.07.2023]

[13] Translation by Author.

> ধ্বংস কৰ ধ্বংস কৰ
> ধনীৰ অহংকাৰ
> দয়া মায়া নকৰিবি
> ক্ষমাৰ দিন যে গল
> হাল, কোৰ, দা, হাতুৰী লৈ
> ৰণলৈ যাওঁ বল । ।[14]

[Destroy, Destroy, The Ego of the rich and elite, Do not show any pity, love and care; The times of forgiveness are now gone, So take your ploughs, hoes, knives, hammers, And, then, let us move towards a war with the elites!][15]

The lines noted above are by Vilas Ghogre, one of the most popular anti-establishment worker-poets from Maharashtra, and Bishnu Prasad Rabha, the firebrand tribal communist rebel from Assam who has been now completely appropriated by the State, respectively. Although both of them come from different regions of the country, the one commonality that they have is that they are often unknown to the contemporary generation of activists and intellectuals – including some who are themselves engaged in cultural movements. With the constant commercialization of the everyday lives of the people, aspects of culture have come to be under the influence of the dehumanizing effects of capitalism. Figures such as Vilas Ghogre and Bishnu Prasad Rabha deserve to be written about. They deserve their own space under the sun where their writings are celebrated and appreciated, but to do that, one needs to first set up a global premise within which their writings are not only appreciated or critiqued but also explore the social conditions under which the songs were written. In this regard, student movements have been exemplary in India. Gone are the days when the radical Indian youth used to be only

---

[14] Lyrics available from https://www.assameselyrical.com/2020/04/bol-bol-bol-lyrics.html [Accessed 28.07.2023]

[15] Translation by Author.

enthralled by Soviet realism,[16] but rather today they have taken up the responsibility of providing voices to innumerable cultural activists from India, who have been deprived of their rightful place in society – especially if they belong to the progressive, socialist, or communist sections of the political spectrum. Socialist imaginings in India were kindled during the 1930s with groups such as the Congress Socialist Party (CSP), the Communist Party of India (CPI) and the Swaraj Party (SP) wanting to work as a pressure group within or with the Indian National Congress (INC) with a view of pushing the mainstream political discourse leftwards.[17] The early Marxists, Socialists and Communists realized the importance of that in India. Cultural movements and protest performances have had a long history in India. The popular saying that 'Indian people like gaana bajana',[18] which today is mostly used to refer to the songs in movies and television dramas, probably stems from the great love that Indians used to possess towards the popular folk traditions in the country. Arun Sen notes:

> Art is the expression of the social emotions of the people and is their offering to the social corporate life. It is inevitably the product of their living and the index of their material well-being. The history of art is an embodiment of this fundamental principle.[19]

The trajectory of cultural protest movements in India has been such that the movement itself has become a manifestation of the different ways in which modernity is witnessed and sought to be experienced in society by a significant section of the population that remains socio-economically and culturally marginalized as is

---

[16] Mishra, P. 'The East was Read'. In V. Prasad (ed), *The East was Read*. New Delhi: Leftword, 2019.

[17] Sarkar, J. 'Power, Hegemony and Politics: Leadership Struggle in the Congress in the 1930s'. *Modern Asian Studies, 40*(2), 2006, 333-70.

[18] Trans. *Singing and Dancing*

[19] Sen, A. 'Art and the Indian People'. In *Marxist Cultural Movement in India, Volume 3: Chronicles and Documents (1943-1964)*. Kolkata: National Book Agency, 1955/2017, p. 335.

evident in the works of many activists who have decided to pen down their analyses, memoirs, and experiences of the cultural movement in India.[20] The tradition of political cultural activism goes back a long way in the subcontinent, especially after 1917 with the Russian Revolution influencing their global counterparts to a large extent even in countries such as the United States and India.[21]

Cultural movements, in many ways, were integral to the development of a sense of modernity in India. The relationship that is shared in India between cultural resistance and modernity can be grasped by a couple of things which can be witnessed, quite unexpectedly one must admit, in India – even within the smaller cities and in the rural areas. The first was a group of people singing Woody Guthrie's song, 'This Land is My Land', and the second was the constant evocation of names such as Pete Seeger, Woody Guthrie, and John Lennon, which is – truth be told - quite unexpected in those social settings that are often dictated by low literacy rates, low human development, and the like. Needless to say, one is referring to the influence of the progressive cultural movement here, which has been a particularly important aspect of the social justice movements in India. No major rally, lockout or strike has ever been conducted that did not have a protest song being sung during them or a protest performance being staged there. These performances in protest sites fulfil a lot of functions within those spaces. Firstly, these performances help the organizers to ensure that the actors engage in the theatrics associated with a strike or protest action. Secondly, they ensure that their demands reach the non-participating masses and the marginalized sections, who often remain unable to grasp the basis and importance of the demands among the protesting masses in simple language. No discussion

---

[20] Rajagopalan, S. *Leave the Disco Dancer Alone: Indian Cinema and Soviet Movie-Going after Stalin*. Delhi: Yoda Press, 2008; Deshpande, S. (ed). *Theatre of the Streets: The Jana Natya Manch Experience*. New Delhi: Janam, 2013; Deshpande, S. 'Socialist Cinema comes to the Rescue'. In V. Prasad (ed), *The East was Read*. New Delhi: Leftword, 2019.

[21] Hashmi, S. 'The First Ten Years of Street Theatre'. In S. Deshpande (ed), *Theatre of the Streets: The Jana Natya Manch Experience*. New Delhi: JANAM, 1988/2013.

about cultural protests and the culture of revolutionary art in the context of India can be complete without considering the rich and varied legacy weaved by organizations such as the Indian Peoples' Theatre Association (IPTA), the Progressive Writers' Association (PWA), Safdar Hashmi Memorial and Trust (SAHMAT), Jana Natya Manch (JANAM), and the like. These organizations have been at the forefront of the progressive cultural movement in the country and have been important forces of social justice in the country. It has often been the case that these organizations have been at the forefront of making the demands of the marginalized of the marginalized heard in the Indian democracy.

In the domain of contemporary student politics, organizations such as the DASTAK, JNU-IPTA, Revolutionary Cultural Front (RCF), the Progressive Theatre Group (PTG), etc. have been important forces. These groups have not only functioned as merely cultural groups within the students' movement but have also proved to be important elements in the ways in which the articulation of the contemporary problems that India faces has been performed ideologically and aesthetically. Many such groups have been instrumental in the negation of the capitalistic false consciousness that reigns in society by bringing forth aspects of realism in their cultural performances – thus staying true to the history of the progressive cultural movement in India22. The first cultural organisation of a progressive kind in India was the Progressive Writers' Association (PWA) which was formed in 1936 under the leadership of Sajjad Zaheer. The PWA was a result of the need felt by writers and activists to organize themselves for the betterment of society as a whole. As Sajjad Zaheer had noted:

> [T]his conference looked at literature not from the point of view of a pedant, as something apart from the rest of life but as a social product, and as such moulded and influenced by the social environment.

---

22 Chattopadhyay, H. 'Writers and the People'. In S. Pradhan (ed.), *Marxist Cultural Movement in India, Volume 3: Chronicles and Documents (1943-1964)*. Kolkata: National Book Agency, 1953/2017; Adorno, T. W. 'On Popular Music'. In J. Storey (ed), Cultural Theory and Popular Culture. London: Prentice Hall, 1992/1998.

Social convulsions did not leave literature alone, and therefore it was the duty of our writers to take account of them, to consciously help through their writings the forces of enlightenment and progress, to struggle against reaction and ignorance in whatever form they may manifest themselves in the society.[23]

Whenever one speaks of cultural resistance, the name that immediately comes to mind is the IPTA because 'With the formation of the IPTA, the project for progressive art, as it got articulated, was threefold as it unfolded: to construct an aesthetic of nationalism or cultural expression grounded in the nation within the Left movement; at the same time, to use the complex 'regional' traditions that cannot get subsumed by a notion of 'nationhood'; while being grounded in a notion of the national even while being expressed in diverse local terms, the emphasis on the radical, seeking to foreground exploitation, whether through colonialism or the structure of Indian society'.[24] The IPTA was formed during the fourth All-India Conference of the PWA which was held from 22-25 May in 1943 at the Marwari Vidyalaya in then Bombay (now Mumbai).[25] It was on the last day of the conference that the IPTA came into being framing its motto: 'People's Theatre Stars the People'.[26] In contemporary India, however, the IPTA has ceased being the force that it once was, with fewer actors and fewer performances being done under its banner. Panikkar notes, 'The progressive cultural movement considered a tumultuous episode in the intellectual history of

---

[23] Zaheer, S. S. A Note on the Progressive Writers' Association. In S. Pradhan (ed.), *Marxist Cultural Movement in India, Volume 1: Chronicles and Documents (1936-1947)*. Kolkata: National Book Agency, 1936/2017, p. 76.

[24] Damodaran, S. People's Music: The Musical Repertoire of the Indian Peoples' Theatre Association. In *The Progressive Cultural Movement: A Critical History*. New Delhi: SAHMAT, 2017, p. 71.

[25] Jalil, R. (2022). 80 Years of IPTA – An Indian Theatre Movement Truly 'For the People'. *The Quint*, May 25. Available at: https://www.thequint.com/voices/opinion/80-years-of-ipta-an-indian-theatre-movement-truly-for-the-people [Accessed 25.07.2023]

[26] Jalil ibid.

India ... has now become a pale shadow of the past. In fact, an all-India movement does not exist anymore., Instead, language-based regional organizations function by claiming the legacy of the earlier all-India movement'.[27]

Even in such a state, groups such as the IPTA, have continued to function in accordance with their most fundamental characteristics, i.e., the exploration of the relationship between modernity and traditions, or in the words of activists, between the modern and the folk traditions of the Indian subcontinent. The relationship between modernism and classicalism, which Zaheer had noted to be one of the foundational elements of the PWA became manifest in the way in which events such as the United Maharashtra People's Theatre Convention were conducted in 1953 where both classical and modern cultural activists and practitioners participated with equal interest.[28] In fact, it is the culmination of the traditional and the modern that has over the course of history become the focal point of the cultural resistance that has characterized numerous rallies, protests, and direct-action movements in contemporary India. Songs and street plays that adhere to the rich legacy of the folk traditions of the country provide the contemporary generations with a window where they can desire to explore the connection that their present holds to the past and the ways in which the relationship comes to define their contemporary socio-political and cultural existence.

Ideological and hegemonic domination cannot be explained only by considering the economic aspects of the society but also need to take into context the ways in which domination is affected by manipulated by cultural modes of domination. Under capitalism, and especially under neoliberalism, culture becomes something that is commercialized and used for hegemonic control over the people reflecting on the tensions that exist

---

[27] Panikkar, K. N. 'Progressive Cultural Movement in India: A Critical Appraisal'. In *The Progressive Cultural Movement: A Critical History*. New Delhi: SAHMAT, 2017, p. 23.

[28] Zaheer op cit.; Unity. (1953/2017). United Maharashtra People's Theatre Convention. In S. Pradhan (ed), *Marxist Cultural Movement in India Volume 2: Chronicles and Documents (1947-1958)*. Kolkata: National Book Agency.

between ideology and politics in the society. The battle between the primacy of ideological consciousness and economic progress is an old one. There is a tendency among most progressive intellectuals and analysts to talk about these two terms in a binary sense pitching one against the other in a way that almost makes it imperative for many to take sides. As the conclusion to the present work will exhibit, this dualistic attitude is not only problematic but also highly dogmatic in character creating unnecessary tensions between various popular modes of protest. Walter Benjamin brought forward the intersections between how the world has been constructed under the aegis and leadership of capital and the manner in which it has been put in the service of the same forces which had formed them, both socio-economically and culturally.[29] Benjamin was speaking here about the power of capital and its global forces which almost convert it into an omnipresent entity in the lives of the people it dominates. Even art, a domain which is often invoked by liberal theorists to be outside the domain of commercial ventures and capital, has become a tool at the hands of capital.[30] Protest songs and other cultural expressions of dissent try to rescue the soul of arts and cultures from such processes of reification that convert society into a one-dimensional one.

The book inspects the many layers of cultural activism within the realm of the students' movement in India. It divides itself into seven chapters. The chapters engage with four critical issues that are being confronted by the radical progressive cultural students' movement. The first is the transformative and transcending nature of cultural politics. This will be followed by an analysis of the relationship between student movements and cultural resistance and why it is important to explore the same. The third chapter will discuss the relationship that cultural movements, especially those that engage students in India, share with the idea of 'modernity', especially taking into cognizance its relevance in the contemporary students' cultural movement in

---

[29] Benjamin, W. (1999). *The Arcades Project.* Trans. H. Eiland & K. McLaughlin. Cambridge Mass.: The Belknap Press of Harvard University Press.

[30] Benjamin, W. Moscow Diary. In *October Volume 35* (pp. 4+9-135). Massachusetts: The MIT Press, 1985.

India and South Asia. The fourth chapter deals with the ways in which cultural activism has continued to thrive in a country dominated by the far-right regime of the BJP. Taking a cue from this, the fifth chapter again discusses the importance of cultural struggles within the students' movements and the ways in which it makes the student movement articulate the internal contradictions of the country. The sixth chapter emphasizes the everyday nature of the cultural struggles of the students, while the seventh chapter focuses on the way in which cultural activism helps student movements to imagine a more subjective attitude towards liberation. The final conclusion engages with the University spaces and the ways in which the cultural movement enables the students to liberate themselves from the technocratic society that promotes half-knowledge and prevents one from getting a holistic and critical view of society.[31]

The society that has come to be under capitalism is a one-dimensional one where human beings are put under a framework where their rationality is being managed by a constant loss of diversity and heterogeneity.[32] The rise of jingoistic nationalism in India is a successor of these processes that become mainstream under capitalism, and especially under neoliberal capitalism. They have created conditions under which radical and progressive voices have been suppressed. Laws have been devised, terms such as 'Urban Naxals'[33] have been invented and fake cases have been manufactured to put intellectuals, artists and citizens asking questions and critiquing the government in jails34 - all in the name of Hindu Khatre mein Hain (Hindus are in Danger). In a situation such as this, one can always remember the Pakistani poet, Habib Jalib who had written:

---

[31] Montag, W. 'The Althusser-Rancière Controversy'. Radical Philosophy, 170, 8-15.

[32] Adorno 1992 op cit., Marcuse, H. *One-Dimensional Man*. London: Routledge and Kegan Paul, 1964/2002.

[33] The word gained immense traction in India since 2018 referring to people in Urban areas who have sympathies towards the Maoist and Naxalite movement. See https://www.indiatoday.in/india-today-insight/story/who-is-an-urban-naxal-1911450-2022-02-10 [Accessed 04.08.2023]

[34] Gupta, A. (ed). *Policing Dissent: 'Urban Naxal' – Myth and Reality*. Kolkata, Rupali, 2019.

ख़तरा है जरदारों को गिरती हुई दीवारों को
सदियों के बीमारों को ख़तरे में इस्लाम नहीं
सारी जमीं को घेरे हुए हैं आख़िर चंद घराने क्यों
नाम नबी का लेने वाले उल्फ़त से बेगाने क्यों
ख़तरा है ख़ूंख़ारों को रंग बिरंगी कारों को
अमरीका के प्यारों को ख़तरे में इस्लाम नहीं
आज हमारे नारों से लज़ी है बया ऐवानों में
बिक न सकेंगे हसरतों अमों ऊँची सजी दुकानों में
ख़तरा है बटमारों को मग़रिब के बाज़ारों को
चोरों को मक्कारों को ख़तरे में इस्लाम नहीं
अम्न का परचम लेकर उठो हर इंसाँ से प्यार करो
अपना तो मंशूर है 'जालिब' सारे जहाँ से प्यार करो
ख़तरा है दरबारों को शाहों के ग़मख़ारों को
नव्वाबों ग़द्दारों को ख़तरे में इस्लाम नहीं[35]

[It is the rich who are in danger; Those who are sick from centuries are in danger, Islam is not in danger; Why is the whole earth occupied by a few individuals; Why are those who take the name of the Prophet robbed off all land and wealth? It is the barbaric ones who are in danger, their colorful cars are in danger, the friends of America are in danger, Islam is not in danger; Today we are proud of our slogans, our desires will not be sold in fancy shops; Today, the Batmars[36] and the markets of the West are in Danger, The thieves and hypocrites are in danger, Islam is not in danger; Rise up with the flag of peace, and love every single human being, a task for which our 'Jalib' is famous all over the world; The courts of the ruling class are in dangers, the Nawabs who are traitors [to the working class] are in danger; Islam is not in danger!][37]

---

[35] Lyrics available from https://www.jakhira.com/2022/02/khatre-me-islam-nahin.html#ixzz88egfa8cg [Accessed 25.07.2023]

[36] Meaning: Those who rob people enroute their journeys.

[37] Translation by author.

Jalib wrote this poem during the days of Zia-ul-Haq's martial law regime in Pakistan. But, if one replaces the word 'Islam' by 'Hindu', one can get a near-perfect description of the state of affairs in India that is dictated by cultural nationalism, jingoism, and neo-fascism. However, the kind of jingoistic nationalism that the Indian far-right under the patronage of the BJP and the RSS has gone far beyond what Zia had achieved in Pakistan even though there are certain similarities between them – especially on the questions of demonizing Faiz Ahmed Faiz and Habib Jalib's poetry. The far-right in India is far more dangerous than Zia-ul-Haq's regime because, unlike the latter which came to power through a military coup and utilized religion only after coming to power, the far-right in India has come to power utilizing civil society, cultural nationalism, majoritarianism and elections whereby their entire existence is based on religious consciousness and hatred towards Muslims, Dalits, and other marginalized sections. The usage of social and democratic measures to suit their own neo-fascist aims that provides them with a certain legitimacy in the eyes of the common masses – even in cases of genocide and rampant structural violence - has converted the Indian far-right into a far more dangerous entity than the Pakistani administrative far-right.

Student movements in recent times have used countless such poems from figures such as Habib Jalin, Faiz Ahmed Faiz and Hemanga Biswas to make their voices heard by the ruling class. The book takes inspiration from such figures in analyzing the importance and relevance of cultural activism for contemporary progressive student activism, and activism for liberation in general. This book does not attempt to be exhaustive scholarly research on the history and ideology of the movements focused on cultural resistance in India. This book instead tries to locate the same in the context of contemporary India emphasizing the new forms of cultural traditions that have emerged in the last decade, especially after the present Narendra Modi-led BJP government came to power in Delhi. This book engages with the internationalist and global nature of the cultural protest movement among Indian students. It deals with the ways in which the cultural movement has dealt with the problems concerning the nation and its people, especially since 2014 – the year when the neo-fascist Modi government first took charge at the centre. Most progressive student organizations consider cultural activism to be one of the major parts of their repertoire because cultural forms of resistance often enable them to make inroads into spaces hitherto deemed out of bounds for many of them.

1
The Transcending Nature of Cultural Protests

অগ্নিযুগৰ ফিৰিঙতি মই নতুন অসম গঢ়িম। নতুন ভাৰত গঢ়িম।
সৰ্বহাৰাৰ সৰ্বস্ব পুনৰ ফিৰাই আনিম নতুন অসম গঢ়িম, নতুন ভাৰত গঢ়িম।
নৱ-কঙ্কালৰ অস্ত্ৰ সাজি, শোষণকাৰীক বধিম।
সৰ্বহাৰাৰ সৰ্বস্ব পুনৰ ফিৰাই আনিম। নতুন অসম গঢ়িম, নতুন ভাৰত গঢ়িম।
ধৰ্ম ব্যৱসায়ীৰ ঠাই নাই তাত। জাতিৰ অহংকাৰ লয় পাব তাত। অস্পৃশ্যতাৰ
মহাদানৱক আপোন হাতেৰে নাশিম। নতুন অসম গঢ়িম। নতুন ভাৰত গঢ়িম।
[...] ভেদাভেদৰ প্ৰাচীৰ ভাঙি সাম্যৰ সৰগ ৰচিম নতুন অসম গঢ়িম। নতুন ভাৰত
গঢ়িম।

- Bhupen Hazarika[38]

[I am a spark of the age of fire. I will build a new Assam[39]; I will build a new India. I will restore everything back to the Proletariat and build a new Assam, a new India. I will make weapons out of the skeletons of the Proletariat and kill the oppressors. I will restore back all the possessions of the poor. I will build a new Assam, a new India. In this new Assam, new India, there will be no place for the merchants of religion. There will be no caste privilege. I will destroy the great demon of untouchability with my own hands.

---

[38] Assamese lyrics available from https://www.assameselyrical.com/2020/02/agni-jugor-firingoti-moi-lyrics.html [Accessed on 28.07.2023]. There is a debate about whether Hazarika had ever said 'I will build a new India', which is not usually available in the lyrics available in general on the internet or in his collected works. However, he did say that, as can be heard from the following recorded version available on YouTube: https://youtu.be/9U2aRsY8APg [Accessed on 09.08.2023]

[39] Hazarika is referring here to his home state, Assam.

> I will build a new Assam, a new India. I will destroy all the walls that divide us and build an equal society. I will build a new Assam, a new India.][40]

In India, one of the common statements that one can hear – on the streets, on television sets, or even on YouTube – is that art, culture and sports should be kept outside the domain and influence of 'politics'. The usage of the term 'politics' here is mostly in a derogatory sense that refers to the kind of meddling that the contemporary BJP government has done with the secular fabric of the nation. There have been cries of boycotting specific movies, books, television shows, etc., and cancel culture has been gaining a lot of ground in contemporary India with mostly Muslim and Progressive cultural figures being at the focal point of such attacks.[41] However, even with such a rampant boycott campaign, the far-right has not been able to completely subvert the secular and transcending nature of the socio-cultural fabric of the Indian subcontinent. This becomes evident in the way in which despite all the political jingoism, *Pathaan*[42] – a film that features Shah Rukh Khan – grossed a revenue of more than 1,000 Crore INR (more than 120 million USD), while the movie *Adipurush*,[43] a film premised on the Hindu epic Ramayana and widely promoted by the far-right before its release turned out to be, in the words of the far-right magazine Swarajya – a major

---

[40] Translation by the author.

[41] Pandit, S. D. 'Cancel Culture and Public Space in India'. The Sunday Guardian, 2023, May 28. Available at: https://sundayguardianlive.com/opinion/cancel-culture-and-public-space-in-india ; Also see https://www.news18.com/news/india/bwood-not-cowed-down-by-threat-against-muslim-actors-293563.html ; https://www.hindustantimes.com/entertainment/bollywood/amid-pathaan-s-success-kangana-ranaut-says-india-is-biased-towards-khans-and-muslim-actors-twitter-users-school-her-101674970534445.html [Accessed 25.07.2023]

[42] See the Wikipedia entry here: https://en.wikipedia.org/wiki/Pathaan_(film) [Accessed 25.07.2023]

[43] See the Wikipedia entry here: https://en.wikipedia.org/wiki/Adipurush [Accessed 25.07.2023]

disaster.[44] The success of *Pathaan* was celebrated by most of secular India as a victory of love over the hate that the BJP is sponsoring across the country[45].

If one takes out the theatrics associated with such an event in the sense that it could give the BJP a temporary setback – because Bollywood is in fact a part of the commercial and cultural machinery that has enabled the BJP to come to power by focusing on the intersections of neoliberalism and majoritarian Hindutva[46] - then the statement does hold ground. Inter-state rivalries have over the course of history affected the ways in which individuals have perceived different societies, people and the cultural traits associated with them. Edward Said, the acclaimed Palestinian social commentator, has shown in great detail how diverse socio-economic and political processes work in tandem to produce multiple layers of marginality within a highly oppressed and exploited community[47]. One can find similar patterns of marginality being analyzed by thinkers who have worked along the terrains of the cultural movement in India. The constant growth of socio-political ideologies based on Islamophobia has aided the construction of the other in India, allowing far-right political formations such as the BJP and the RSS to garner tremendous amounts of support from the general populace. Such a brand of right-wing populism and the kind of support that the far-right has managed to amass has gripped the nation and is hitherto unheard of in Indian history. However, if one goes by the words of Habib Jalib, one should not be surprised at all. Quoting Jalib's poem Musheer at this point might be pertinent:

---

[44] See https://swarajyamag.com/culture/future-of-bollywood-after-the-disaster-that-is-adipurush [Accessed 25.07.2023]

[45] See https://timesofindia.indiatimes.com/india/pathaans-success-shows-indians-want-love-not-hate/articleshow/97442084.cms?from=mdr [Accessed 25.07.2023]

[46] HM, S. K. 'Constructing the Nation's Enemy: "Hindutva", popular culture and the Muslim 'other' in Bollywood cinema'. *Third World Quarterly*, 34(3), 2013, 458–469.

[47] Said, E. 'Dignity, Solidarity and the Penal Colony'. In E. Said, *On Palestine*. New Delhi: Leftword, 2001/2014.

मैं ने उस से ये कहा, ये जो दस करोड़ हैं, जहल का निचोड़ हैं, उन की फ़िक्र सो गई
हर उमीद की किरन, ज़ुल्मतों में खो गई, ये ख़बर दुरुस्त है, उन की मौत हो गई
बे-शुऊर लोग हैं, ज़िंदगी का रोग हैं, और तेरे पास है, उन के दर्द की दवा
मैं ने उस से ये कहा, तू ख़ुदा का नूर है, अक़्ल है शुऊर है, क़ौम तेरे साथ है
तेरे ही वजूद से, मुल्क की नजात है, तू है महर-ए-सुब्ह-ए-नौ, तेरे बाद रात है
बोलते जो चंद हैं, सब ये शर-पसंद हैं, उन की खींच ले ज़बाँ, उन का घोंट दे गला।
मैं ने उस से ये कहा।
जिन को था ज़बाँ पे नाज़, चुप हैं वो ज़बाँ-दराज़, चैन है समाज में, बे-मिसाल फ़र्क़ है
कल में और आज में, अपने ख़र्च पर हैं क़ैद, लोग तेरे राज में, आदमी है वो बड़ा,
दर पे जो रहे पड़ा, जो पनाह माँग ले, उस की बख़्श दे ख़ता, मैं ने उस से ये कहा
[...] दस करोड़ ये गधे, जिन का नाम है अवाम, क्या बनेंगे हुक्मराँ
तू "यक़ीं" है ये "गुमाँ", अपनी तो दुआ है ये, सद्र तू रहे सदा
मैं ने उस से ये कहा। 48

[I said this to him, These hundred million are the ones who personify the epitome of ignorance, Their conscience has gone to a deep slumber, Every ray of hope is lost in the darkness, This news is true, they are the living dead, Completely mindless, A disease of life And you hold in your hands the cure for their ills. You are the light of God, Wisdom and knowledge personified, The nation is with you. It is only through your grace that the nation can be saved, You are the light of a new morning after you there is only night; The few who speak out are all mischief makers; You should tear out their tongues, You should throttle their throats. Those who were once proud of their tongues are now silent, their tongues are tied, and there is peace in the society. There is an unmatched difference between the past and the present. These people are imprisoned at their own expense under your rule. Only those people who are doing good who are lying at your door, who seek shelter from you, you forgive him. I said this to him. These 10 Crore stupid people, whom we call the 'people'. What will they become rulers as they are now convinced that all is

---

48 Hindi lyrics are available from Rekhta.org at: https://www.rekhta.org/nazms/mushiir-main-ne-us-se-ye-kahaa-habib-jalib-nazms?lang=hi

lost? I only ask you to remain faithful that change is possible. I said this to him.]49

Like the then Pakistan, India too is at the cusp of falling into a militarized dictatorial regime and is being ruled by political figure(s) with a fetish for jingoistic nationalism, authoritarianism, and anti-minority hatred. The recent surge of cultural activism in India challenging the cultural nationalism of the BJP[50] has exhibited that it is possible to completely counter the constructed other. It becomes particularly manifested within the realm of cultural resistance because cultural activism in India has mostly been associated with the broader South Asian society. It has often been the case that cultural activism in India has overlapped or has taken inspiration from the cultural activists from both Bangladesh and Pakistan. Although the influence of the same has largely been restricted to the eastern and northern regions, it cannot be denied that progressive poets and lyricists from across the borders have exerted a considerable influence on the cultural movement in the country as well.[51] The general hostility that one sees in the eyes of the people on the mention of the word 'Pakistan', changes completely when one starts talking about the progressive Urdu poetry which took root in Pakistan after the partition of British India in 1947. The names of people such as Faiz Ahmed Faiz and Habib Jalib are as much revered in India, as they are in Pakistan. This is in spite of the fact that

> Over the decades, instead of resolving the [disputes], we created more issues and more cleavages. Resultantly, we fought wars, went nuclear and tried to undermine each other at all levels with the implacable mutual hostility

---

[49] Original Urdu lyrics are available from https://qausain.wordpress.com/2009/11/07/musheer/ . [Accessed 25.07.2023] Translation has been modified by the author. The last paragraph is an original translation by the author.

[50] Menon, S. 'From National Culture to Cultural Nationalism'. In *On Nationalism*. New Delhi: Aleph, 2016.

[51] Jalil, R. *Liking Progress, Loving Change: A Literary History of the Progressive Writers' Movement in Urdu*. New Delhi: Oxford University Press, 2020.

continuing to be the major impediment in fostering regional cooperation'.[52]

Amidst such an environment of hostility, cultural resistance, and modes of protest, in many ways, has helped the individuals engaged in the process of constructing stronger socio-cultural democratic processes, to build a strong connection between theory and praxis. It has enabled them to transcend the narrow confines placed by the jingoistic nationalism practised and rendered mainstream by the contemporary ruling bloc in the country.[53] This is most evidently noticed in the case of how poets from Pakistan have become prominent voices of dissent in India against far-right domination. During the 2016 protest movement at JNU that stemmed from the allegations made by the BJP government against some students as being seditious and threats to the security of the country,[54] along with poets such as Pash and Gorakh whose names make them look a part of the framework of Hindu India despite them being miles away from the same ideologically,[55] Muslim poets from Pakistan such as Faiz and Jalib too had been a constant feature.

Renditions of their iconic poems have gone on to become the symbols of the movement. Such events are not surprising considering that India has had a long history of cultural resistance that also gets bolstered by the fact that the civilizational values which India has inherited also go back thousands of years and are shared with its immediate neighbours

---

[52] Basit, A. *Hostility: A Diplomat' Diary on Pakistan India Relations*. Karachi: Lightstone Publishers, 2021, p. 14.

[53] Salam, Z. U. 'Jingoism as Politics'. Frontline, February 22, 2021. Available at: https://frontline.thehindu.com/cover-story/politics-post-pulwama-balakot-airstrike-modi-muscular-nationalism-chest-thumping-jingoism/article33895993.ece [Accessed 25.07.2023]

[54] See https://economictimes.indiatimes.com/news/politics-and-nation/who-are-members-of-tukde-tukde-gang-rti/articleshow/73263876.cms [Accessed 25.07.2023]. For more details, one can refer to Kumar. K. *Bihar to Tihar: My Political Journey*. New Delhi: Juggernaut, 2019.

[55] See https://scroll.in/article/923098/reading-gorakh-pandey-the-peoples-poet-who-rebelled-against-his-feudal-roots [Accessed 04.08.2023]

– something that the Radcliffe line[56] has found it difficult to completely erase off. It is true that the heretical tendencies which are dominant in contemporary India are the root cause of a lot of issues which are pertinent in modern-day India, but at the same time, it is also true that traditions are rooted in the history of a nation. The relationship between traditions, history and the state of contemporary affairs is a complicated one, and it affects the state of modernity in different societies differently.

When events such as 'Nights of Resistance' or 'Occupy the Night' are organized on Indian campuses, these contradictions come out in the open. Organizing cultural events at night is often a calculated strategy that many organizations adopt to not only make their voices heard but also to assert their positions on certain aspects of life under contemporary capitalism. These activities make the activists question the appropriation of their cultural characteristics by the ruling ideas that are so common under mainstream capitalism.[57] The usage of 'Night' in most of these events deserves special attention because it is often used to signify the growing loss of security that women face on Indian campuses - due to increased cases of sexual harassment, eve-teasing, etc. – and in society in general.[58] Activists analyze the importance of the 'Night' in these ways:

> We can do these events during the day as well. But we do at night because we want to make a point. Women in India still fear to go out alone at night,

---

[56] Radcliffe Line is the border drawn up by the British Authorities to demarcate India and Pakistan (including both West and East Pakistan). For more details refer to https://www.pritikachowdhry.com/post/partition-of-india-radcliffe-line [Accessed 25.07.2023]

[57] McRobbie, A. 'Post-Marxism and Cultural Studies: A Post-Script'. In L. Grossberg, C. Nelson, & P. Treichler (eds), *Cultural Studies*. New York: Routledge, 1992.

[58] Mishra, M. "Only when a daughter is Safe, She'll be able to Study'. Interview by S. Chakraborty. In S. Chakraborty & P. Ambedkar (eds), *Students Won't be Quiet*. New Delhi: Leftword, 2022; N., J. S. 'A Fight for Gender Justice: Paving the Path for Progressive Politics at Pondicherry University'. In S. Chakraborty & P. Ambedkar (eds), *Students Won't be Quiet*. New Delhi: Leftword, 2022; Das, S. 'Breaking Silence: Shubh Laxmi's Struggle in Assam'. In S. Chakraborty & P. Ambedkar (eds), *Students Won't be Quiet*. New Delhi: Leftword, 2022.

> even when they go out with male friends or relatives, they are at risk – both from the society and from the ones with whom they go out with. When we do these events at night, it sends out a message. It speaks about the fact that women are equal in the society, and that they deserve as much space during the night as men have. (Student Activist, Delhi)

> The politics of 'Night' is a twofold one. Firstly, it shows that women have as much right and as much authority to be out at night and if a society is failing to ensure secured conditions for the same, then the society itself is failing. Secondly, when one organizes women to sing and dance and act at night, we are not only attacking the idea that women cannot go out at night, we are also putting up that they not only can go out but also sing, dance and act during night. This is especially important in a country like ours where such activities were once seen to be out of bounds for women, mainly for women coming from so-called good families. (Student Activist, Guwahati)

The restriction placed on women from coming out in the open performing has been a historical hurdle that organizations such as the IPTA have been struggling against.[59] Student politics and cultural activism in contemporary India have often acted as complementary forces to each other to address such issues. Campus spaces occupy an important position in that regard because they not only provide space to diverse political tendencies but also do so in a manner which nurtures these voices, at least ideally. The kind of space, which is harbored by educational institutions, especially the publicly funded ones in India, is such that they create the necessary conditions under which the students can engage with diverse ideas and thoughts, many of which might run antithetical to the traditional norms. It

---

[59] Singh, L. 'Transgression of Boundaries: Women of IPTA'. In *The Progressive Cultural Movement: A Critical History*. New Delhi: SAHMAT, 2017.

is the inherent quality of student movements that it can construct an alternative space for practicing its politics, even if that is temporary in nature. And space plays quite an important role in the overall aura that a theatre or a performance produces often increasing its impact on the audience.[60] The separation that exists between the actors and the audience within a professional theatre space is not there in the case of theatre or cultural activities that take place in the streets, especially within university spaces. Students have a much better chance of engaging with actors in cultural troupes operating within a university than they have with actors and technicians of the plays that take place within the aegis of professional theatre. The interaction that the students have, especially those coming from the marginalized sections of society, with actors often means an engagement they have with the ideas represented in the play because plays focused on social justice and liberation – the ones which are usually performed within the campuses - are not only about the actors or about the techniques and props used in them but rather they have become about the ideas represented in them. The basic points that activists elaborate on make one appreciate the role that cultural protests and modes of expression play in the overall propagation of ideas and progressive politics in society. One activist reflected:

> Cultural resistance is an important part of the framework of socio-political resistance, both in the society and on the campus. When we perform a play, it is less about the techniques used but more about the ideas represented in them. When I direct a play, I make sure that the actors know what they are performing and are not just reciting the lines. So, when people come to talk to them, they not only discuss about the play but also the issue addressed by the play, or the social dynamics reflected in them. (Student Cultural Activist, Delhi)

---

[60] Carlson, M. 'Whose Space is it, Anyway?'. In B. K. Becker & S. McCarroll (eds.), *Theatre and Space*. Tuscaloosa: The University of Alabama Press, 2016.

Political theatre and cultural politics are not new things – as against the dominant narrative that many of the intellectuals and activists of the far-right would have the world believe.[61] One of the most important cultural activists from India, Safdar Hashmi noted back in the late 1980s:

> Street Theatre, as it is known today, can trace its direct lineage no further than the years immediately after the Russian Revolution in 1917. ... [The Period witnessed] the beginning of a new kind of agitprop theatre performed on the streets, at factory gates, markets, dockyards, playgrounds, barnyards and so on. Avowedly political in nature, this theatre sought its audiences at their places of work or stay rather than attempting to bring them to the theatre hall.[62]

Street theatre, or for that matter any form of progressive cultural activism, thus, is not only a method of bringing up issues but also a prominent strategy through which students, intellectuals and workers come into interaction with each other creating a dialectical and interconnected network of thought and practices to enable the reoccupation of the space under capitalism. The movement for the re-occupation of space under capitalism, again, is often linked to the ways in which different aspects of the individual's life are dominated by the material and ideological forces of finance capital and the far right. These conditions construct a one-dimensional social reality where the idea of transcendence itself is often restricted to mere reforms or in most cases, rendered impossible. The complete marginalization of the human potential produces an exploitative social reality where the human potential of individuals gets completely subdued by

---

[61] Karnad, R. 'How Extreme Student Protests launched Narendra Modi's Career'. The Wire, December 16, 2019. Available at: https://thewire.in/politics/student-protests-narendra-modi-politics-career-navnirman-movement [Accessed 25.07.2023]

[62] Hashmi, S. 'The Tradition of Street Theatre'. In *The Right to Perform: Selected Writings of Safdar Hashmi*. New Delhi: SAHMAT, 1986/1989, p. 6.

channels of capitalist dehumanization.[63] Under such circumstances, it is often strategies based on direct action that have come to be the most effective method of engaging with the state. One activist states:

> Cultural activism is an extremely important part of the overall framework of resistance in the country. After neoliberalism, a lot of people, students especially, have been completely divorced from their roots. Being divorced from their roots makes them completely susceptible to the forces of neoliberalism. Through the cultural movement, we can at least bring some of them closer to their roots, make them understand and analyze the same and then use the same to analyze their present. That is a classical Marxist method of doing things. (Student Cultural Activist, Bengaluru)

Cultural activism, as can be inferred from the statement, often becomes a central element in all direct-action movements because it provides a platform for non-political actors (not used here in a theatrical sense) to become active politically.[64] This translates to broader alliances being made – something that is of utmost importance considering the situation that India faces with regard to the fascistic rise of the BJP and the constant threat to its internal democratic structure and secular ethos. Cultural activism within the campuses is important here because it is not only a method of criticism – both of mainstream art and society – but rather it proposes an alternative form and content, one that is often more participatory and radical than mainstream forms and content of art.[65] It is a process through which students initiate

---

[63] Marcuse 1964 op cit.; Bailes, J. Consciousness and the Neoliberal Subject: A Theory of Ideology via Marcuse, Jameson and Zizek. London: Routledge, 2020.

[64] *Burbank*, C. 'Ladies against Women: Theatre Activism and Satirical Gender Play in the 1980s'. In J. C. Countryman (ed), *Theatre and Politics in the Twentieth Century*. Tuscaloosa: The University of Alabama Press, 2016.

[65] Premchand, M. 'The Nature and Purpose of Literature'. In S. Pradhan (ed), *Marxist Cultural Movement in India: Chronicles and Documents (1936-1947): Volume 1*. Kolkata: National Book Agency, 1979/2017, pp. 79-80.

the realignment and re-engineering of the spaces within the campuses, which are although theoretically supposed to be democratic in nature are often only so by their definition. In reality, they are often dominated by the ideological state apparatuses that not only exploit their bodies but also their very sociocultural existence.

Under the kind of neo-fascist regime that one has in India, ideological state apparatuses also transform into repressive state apparatuses. There is no proper distinction between them in India if one considers their usage against the marginalized populace. The distinction that Althusser constructed between the Ideological State Apparatuses (ISAs) and the Repressive State Apparatuses (RSAs) was one that was constructed by the methods through which they interfered with the society – primarily based on whether they did so within the realm of ideology or repression.[66] In the context of India, both these aspects have fused with each other such that ideological repression (say based on religion) has become synonymous with coercive violent repression that can be witnessed in the proliferation of religious exclusion, communalism, and the like.

Student movements find it easier to overcome the fault lines caused by these issues than the full-fledged political movements of the day. This is not only because student movements are often free from the burden of political correctness that characterizes the mainstream political activities of the day. For example, while mainstream politics often has to remain bound within the contours of political correctness, cultural modes of expression find it a lot easier to transcend the boundaries put in place by such social norms. Take the case of the Justice for Rohith Movement, a radical anti-caste movement that stemmed from the social boycott of five Dalit students at the University of Hyderabad that resulted in the institutional murder of one activist among the five, Rohith Vemula, whose name has become

---

[66] Althusser, L. *Lenin and Philosophy and Other Essays*. New York: Monthly Review Press, 1974.

synonymous with the anti-caste movement in India.[67] The movement quickly gained national prominence with members of the global civil society coming on to join the movement. The reasons for this quick escalation of the movement to national prominence lie not only in the fact that a bright Dalit scholar had been forced to take his own life[68] but also because student movements are based on within students' movements, one finds it relatively easier to bring forward ideas and thoughts which may not have a direct ideological and/or geographical connection with the space within which the movement is being conducted. Issues such as the ideological contours of women's liberation, often do not get the kind of attention that they deserve in mainstream politics. While within the field of politics in a civic sense, women's liberation has been restricted to a mere evocation of policy reforms and certain bureaucratic reforms, student politics has questioned the various ways in which policy reforms have failed to address the social inequalities in place. It is specifically within this domain that cultural resistance remains a highly relevant model of expressing dissent against social injustices in society. While the mainstream political discourse often works on the assumption that the marginalized population needs to be led, the cultural resistance model transforms them into leaders themselves with their voices being represented and amplified in a manner with which they themselves are most comfortable.

The purpose of radical progressive art is that it reflects the social reality as it exists which makes it different from the art that is usually practised by those coming from privileged socio-economic and cultural backgrounds.[69] The kind of cultural resistance that students have been putting up speaks truth to the forces of power in the sense that they challenge the dominant logic of homogenization and segmentation that becomes

---

[67] Singh, K., K. P., Z., & Deb Roy, S. 'Justice for Rohith Vemula: Watershed Moment within the Anti-Caste Students' Movement'. In S. Chakraborty & P. Ambedkar (eds.), *Students Won't be Quiet*. New Delhi: Leftword, 2022.

[68] Singh et al. ibid.

[69] Ali, A. 'Progressive View of Art'. In S. Pradhan (ed), *Marxist Cultural Movement in India: Chronicles and Documents (1936-1947): Volume 1*. Kolkata: National Book Agency, 1979/2017.

mainstream under capitalism, and which completely subverts the idea of radical individualism and development of one's own organic personality.[70] In other words, their models of resistance through their emphasis on issues such as security, basic facilities, and accommodation have interfered with and addressed the problems faced by people – students and otherwise – in their everyday lives. The ability of the cultural resistance model to make inroads into the everyday lives of the people is the major revolutionary quality of any practical or theoretical paradigm. The everyday nature makes it able to locate itself within the concrete reality that people must face in their everyday lives through which they shape and get shaped by the space around them.[71] The power of locating one's art within the concrete reality is what is exhibited by the great socialist folk songs of people such as Hemanga Biswas, who along with his troupe[72] transformed figures such as Paul Robeson from the United States into household names in regions such as Assam, one of the highly underdeveloped regions of India:

ওরা আমাদের গান গাইতে দেয়না
নিগ্রো ভাই আমার পল রবসন
আমরা আমাদের গান গাই ওরা চায়না।।

ওরা ভয় পেয়েছে রবসন
আমাদের রক্ত চোখকে ভয় পেয়েছে
আমাদের দৃপ্ত কণ্ঠে ভয় পেয়েছে
আমাদের কুচকাওয়াজে ভয় পেয়েছে রবসন
ওরা বিপ্লবের ডাঙ্করুতে ভয় পেয়েছে রবসন।।

ওরা ভয় পেয়েছে জীবনের
ওরা ভয় পেয়েছে মরণের

---

[70] Horkheimer, M., & Adorno, T. W. *Dialectic of Enlightenment*. Stanford: Stanford University Press, 1944/2016.

[71] Lefebvre, H. *The Production of Space*. London: Blackwell, 1994; Chattopadhyaya, D. P. *Science and Philosophy in Ancient India*. New Delhi: Aakar, 2013.

[72] There have been certain views, which have argued that Biswas' songs need to be attributed to his whole troupe and not just to him.

ওরা ভয় করে সেই স্মৃতিকে
ওরা ভয় পেয়েছে দুঃস্বপনে।

ওরা ভয় পেয়েছে রবসন
জনতার কলোচ্ছাসে ভয় পেয়েছে
একতার তীব্রতায় ভয় পেয়েছে
হিম্মতের শক্তিতে ভয় পেয়েছে রবসন
ওরা সংহারের মূর্তি দেখে ভয় পেয়েছে রবসন|[73]

[They don't allow us to raise our voice; My negro brother Paul Robeson; We sing in our raised voice. They don't like, they don't like, My negro brother Paul Robeson; They're fear-struck Robeson, They're fear-struck as they hear our war cry, They're fear-struck as they see our red eye, They're fear-struck as they feel our bravery, Robeson, My negro brother Paul Robeson; They are afraid of living, They are afraid of the dead, They are afraid of remembering, They are afraid of those dreams; They are afraid Robeson. They are afraid of the People's Movement, They are afraid of our Unity, They are afraid of our Courage, They are afraid of their own demise][74]

---

[73] Lyrics available from http://banglaygaan.blogspot.com/2008/05/negro-bhai-amar-paul-robson.html [Accessed 26.03.2023]

[74] Part translation by Deepankar Choudhury (See http://anondogaan.blogspot.com/2014/11/paul-robeson-lyrics-translation.html [Accessed 26.07.2023]). Some parts of the translation have been amended by the author for better readability. The last three lines translated by the author.

2
Students' Rebellions and the Cultural Movement

भड़क रहे हैं आग लब-ए नग़मगर से हम
खामोश क्या रहेंगे जमाने के डर से हम
ले दे के अपने पास फ़कत एक नज़र तो है
क्यों देखें जिंदगी को किसी की नजर से हम
माना के इस ज़मीन को ना गुलज़ार कर सके
कुछ खार कम तो कर दिये, गुजरे जिधर से हम!
—Sahir Ludhianvi[1]

[Here we go, stoking fire through song-laden lips, The fear of the world can never staunch the flow of our words. In all, we have just one view, our own. Why should we see the world through someone else's eyes? It is true, we did not turn the world into a garden. But at least we lessened some thorns from the paths we travelled]

Subjective experiences are a major part of the students' movement, as well as of the cultural movement, as they constitute the connection that exists between local circumstances and broader ideological issues.[2] This connection is vital because it is through how one experiences society that one constitutes one's social being.[3] One's self-identification and subjective understanding of one's own self make one aware of the various

---

[1] Mir, A. H., & Mir, R. *Anthems of Resistance: A Celebration of Progressive Urdu Poetry*. New Delhi: Roli Books, 2006, p. 1.

[2] Inglis, F. *Cultural Studies*. London: Blackwell, 1993.

[3] Thompson, E. P. *The Making of the English Working Class*. London: Vintage, 1968/2013.

forms of exploitation that one is subjected to. However, it is often the case that individuals do not possess the necessary language to articulate the same which puts them at a disadvantage, even at times within the progressive movement.[4] The state and the ruling class retain some control over both forms of mass and popular culture in the society which makes the task of developing a truly democratic and people's form of cultural resistance extremely difficult.[5] Thus, it becomes extremely important to analyze the language and techniques that are used to produce cultural artifacts within the progressive cultural movement that is often done to ensure that the meaning of the cultural artifact is as close as possible to the one actually intended.[6]

The basic challenge for any cultural movement remains the usage of 'the everyday culture of the oppressed [and take] the signs of that which oppresses them and [use] them for its own purposes'.[7] Doing this entails within itself to take note of the various kinds of subjectivities that get expressed in the everyday lives of marginalized and exploited people. The students' cultural movement has often engaged with such topics in a manner which have been far more radical and everyday in nature than mainstream politics has ever done. This has made them a vital force in the Indian democracy. This vitality was expressed by two student activists who argued about the centrality of the mass nature of the students' cultural movement and the importance of the same within the contemporary socio-cultural situation of the country:

> Through our cultural protests, we express the dissatisfaction that students have with how their everyday lives are managed within the campus. For example, we once did a play on how the campus

---

[4] Achrar, D., & Panikkar, S. K. (eds.), *Articulating Resistance: Art and Activism*. New Delhi: Tulika Books, 2012.

[5] Ghosh, A. '"Meanings" of the Revolution: Language in the Street Plays of the Jana Natya Manch'. In S. Deshpande (ed), *Theatre of the Streets: The Jana Natya Manch Experience*. New Delhi: JANAM, 2013.

[6] Ibid.

[7] Fiske, J. 'The Culture of Everyday Life'. In L. Grossberg, C. Nelson, & P. Treichler (eds), *Cultural Studies*. New York: Routledge, 1992, p. 157.

had no water. The play reverberated so much among the students that we had to do a repeat performance a few weeks later. That is because the students felt something there that they could relate to. This is very important because it brings us back to our concrete reality, which is important since most of the time we talk about universal terms such as social justice, liberation, etc., which are important but are not tangible enough for many to relate to in their everyday lives for a variety of reasons. Through cultural protests, we are doing this job of relating them. (Student Cultural Activist, Delhi)

The way in which we can address issues through our cultural protests is far more ordinary in nature than how we do that in general student politics. Take the case of a very ordinary issue such as the buildings breaking down all over the campus. In a protest, how we can address this is very formal and will follow a representation, a protest and a discussion. But in a cultural protest, we can be a lot more innovative, we can dress up somebody as a building and make the person talk. This innovative nature of cultural protests not only makes them attractive but also makes them different from the abstract utopian ideological battles that student movements are often engaged in daily. In some ways, this enhances our experience of ideology because then we can actually see its relevance in real life, or imagine it. (Student Cultural Activist, Guwahati)

However, as these activists point out, student politics in India also run the perennial risk of entrapping itself within certain forms of utopianism—often symbolized by the kind of idealism in one's everyday life that seems achievable within the campus spaces. They often have the tendency to dive into the dynamics of what they want to assert rather than focusing on the actually existing state of things—aspects that were part of Marx's critique of the Utopian Socialists of his times.[8] This can sometimes result in the movements getting completely disconnected from the political reality that confronts most of the people in the society. While most student activists continue to hold on steadfastly to their ideological and political beliefs, it is true that those beliefs might not always be in synchronization with the social reality that they live through in their everyday lives. In these circumstances, cultural activism enables them to remain connected to the world outside the campus because its premise is based on the idea that '[o]nly that art, which is the outcome of the highest consciousness, which reflects the social reality, is progressive... [it is] a direct outcome of the consciousness of our material and actual existence'.[9] This can be explained by carefully analyzing how poets such as Faiz and Jalib have found spaces on Indian campuses. During the recent wave of student movements in the country and during the anti-CAA protests, these poets have become the voice of the resistance. The poem which was at the center of attention was a poem by Faiz, Hum Dekhenge, which went like this:

हम देखेंगे; लाज़िम है कि हम भी देखेंगे;
वो दिन कि जिसका वादा है
जो लोह-ए-अज़ल में लिखा है; जब ज़ुल्म-ओ-सितम के कोह-ए-गरां
रुई की तरह उड़ जाएँगे; हम महकूमों के पाँव तले
ये धरती धड़-धड़ धड़केगी; और अहल-ए-हकम के सर ऊपर; जब बिजली
कड़-कड़ कड़केगी;
जब अर्ज़-ए-ख़ुदा के काबे से सब बुत उठवाए जाएँगे; हम अहल-ए-सफ़ा,
मरदूद-ए-हरम मसनद पे बिठाए जाएँगे;
सब ताज उछाले जाएँगे, सब तख़्त गिराए जाएँगे
बस नाम रहेगा अल्लाह का, जो ग़ायब भी है हाज़िर भी
जो मंज़र भी है नाज़िर भी
उड़ेगा अन-अल-हक़ का नारा

---

[8] Paden, R. 'Marx's Critique of the Utopian Socialists'. *Utopian Studies, 13*(2), 2000, 67-91.

[9] Ali op cit., p. 95.

जो मैं भी हूँ और तुम भी हो; और राज़ करेगी खुल्क-ए-खुदा; जो मैं भी हूँ और तुम भी हो।[10]

[We will see! We are all duty-bound to see what happens on the promised day that is carved in stone in history, We will see! When cruelty and tyranny will be blown off to great heights like fluffs of cotton; When the progressing steps of the marching downtrodden people will make the earth beneath their feet shake and shudder, When the skies above the heads of tyrant rulers are split by streaks of lightning, We will see! When the idols of false Gods will be uprooted from the sacred square of the Kaaba,[11] When the Power will be granted to the marginalized. All the crowns of the powerful will be tossed up in the air, and all the thrones will be ground to dust, We will see! Only the name of Allah will prevail, the Allah who is invisible and yet omnipresent, who is the scene and its viewer. Then the cry of 'I am the truth' will echo throughout the skies, which includes both you and I!][12]

These lines do not only go on to analyze the state of affairs in the then Pakistani society but also provide the listeners with the zeal to alter it along with a vision for the post-capitalist future—one of the most fundamental reasons behind its constant evocation in countries such as India. It goes without saying that the poem, despite it being written in 1978 in Pakistan—a year after the imposition of martial law in Pakistan, is as much relevant in

---

[10] Lyrics have been sourced from Kavitakosh. Available at: shorturl.at/AFNT7 [Accessed 25.07.2023]

[11] Kaaba refers to the sacred budling of Mecca. See https://www.merriam-webster.com/dictionary/Kaaba#:~:text=Kaaba-,noun,which%20Muslims%20turn%20in%20praying [Accessed 08.08.2023]

[12] Translated by the author.

contemporary India as it was in the then Pakistan.[13] Sung by the legendary Iqbal Bano draped in a saree in protest against the law passed against women wearing Sarees during the dictatorial regime of General Zia-ul-Haq in Pakistan, this poem of Faiz has since become a symbol of anti-establishment politics in South Asia. Naturally, students during many of their protest movements, be it at the FTII, in the IISC, or in JNU or in HCU, have taken up this song to voice their concerns[14]—to make the ruling class aware of the injustices that they have been inflicting on the students and the society in general in the name of national development and civilizational upliftment. The far-right in India raised a storm over the fact that Faiz uses the word 'Allah' here they equated it with the potential Islamization of the Indian society[15] that the far-right regularly uses to rally hatred against Muslims in the country. They, quite naturally, equated Faiz with Pakistan, and 'Allah' with radical Islam, and then went on to penalize the students engaged in its rendition in reputed institutions such as the Indian Institute of Technology, Kanpur (IITK), the Indian Institute of Management, Ahmedabad (IIM-A), the Indian Institute of Science, Bengaluru (IISC), etc.[16] The far-right in the country left no stone unturned to demonize not only the poets associated with the poems but also those who

---

[13] Mankotia, A. 'India Still Sings This Pak Singer's Songs: Remembering Iqbal Bano'. The Quint, 2021, April 21. Available at: https://www.thequint.com/opinion/pakistani-singer-iqbal-bano-legacy-delhi-gharana-faiz-songs-of-protest-general-zia-hum-dekhenge-india#:~:text=In%201978%2C%20a%20year%20after,Arts%20Council%20on%2013%20February [Accessed 25.07.2023]

[14] SAHMAT. *In Dark Times: Voices against Intolerance*. New Delhi: SAHMAT, 2016; All India Convention of Students' Struggles. *New Wave of Student Movements in India: Stories of Resistance from Indian Campuses*. Bengaluru: All India Forum for Right to Education, 2017.

[15] See https://scroll.in/latest/948664/we-will-not-determine-if-faizs-poem-hum-dekhenge-is-anti-hindu-clarifies-iit-kanpur , https://www.deccanherald.com/national/national-politics/hum-dekhenge-poem-row-lyrics-that-stirred-controversy-791054.html ; https://indianexpress.com/article/trending/trending-in-india/students-singing-faiz-ahmads-hum-dekhenge-at-14000ft-goes-viral-6200607/

[16] See https://swarajyamag.com/blogs/i-am-the-faculty-who-opposed-faizs-hum-dekhenge-in-iit-kanpur-campus-and-here-is-why-i-did-it [Accessed 25.07.2023]

celebrate and study the poems. However, in doing so, the ruling fractions have completely forgotten that the cultural movement in India has historically been a highly internationalist one. It has never been restricted to Indian cultural figures, or even to poets and artists from South Asia. Rather, it has a long history of associating itself with radical voices from across the globe. Take the example of Woody Guthrie's iconic song, 'This land is Your Land' or the civil rights anthem 'We Shall Overcome', which has come to occupy almost an iconic status in India. It is sung in most radical meetings across the country with the song being translated into almost all the major languages in India. Two activists recounted their experiences with the particular iconic song:

> We sang this song everywhere. On the streets, in our conferences, in the classrooms. Now we understand that the lyrics or words used in the song are alien to many who listen to it, but it is the essence that touches them. (Student Activist, Assam)

> The internationalism that progressive student movements have come to embrace in the country gets reflected through our celebration of these songs. When we sing songs such as We Shall Overcome, we are not only speaking of us but rather we are talking and taking a pledge to fight for the liberation of all human beings all over the globe. (Student Activist, Telangana)

This statement reveals the deep tentacles of the cultural movement in the country, with many activists finding cultural activism to be one of the primary vehicles through which they ensure the survival of their ideological politics in a society, that has since the early 1990s continued to move towards embracing far-right politics. Although it might be falling into the realm of idealism and metaphysics if one says that artists and writers are affected more by the changes in society than other people, it is true that they do get affected, but they are successful in expressing their views about the same in a different manner than others. In other words, cultural activists more than being differently affected by these changes, often possess the ability to express the issues in a different manner. For example, one can take the example of Habib Jalib's poem 'Zulmat ko Zia':

इक हश्र बपा है घर में दम घुटता है गुम्बद-ए-बे-दर में
इक शख़्स के हाथों मुद्दत से रुस्वा है वतन दुनिया-भर में
ऐ दीदा-वरो इस ज़िल्लत को क़िस्मत का लिखा क्या लिखना
ज़ुल्मत को ज़िया सरसर को सबा बंदे को ख़ुदा क्या लिखना
लोगों पे ही हम ने जाँ वारी की हम ने ही उन्हीं की ग़म-ख़्वारी
होते हैं तो हों ये हाथ क़लम शाएर न बनेंगे दरबारी
इब्लीस-नुमा इंसानों की ऐ दोस्त सना क्या लिखना
ज़ुल्मत को ज़िया सरसर को सबा बंदे को ख़ुदा क्या लिखना
हक़ बात पे कोड़े और ज़िंदाँ बातिल के शिकंजे में है ये जाँ
इंसाँ हैं कि सहमे बैठे हैं ख़ूँ-ख़्वार दरिंदे हैं रक़्साँ
इस ज़ुल्म-ओ-सितम को लुत्फ़-ओ-करम इस दुख को दवा क्या लिखना
ज़ुल्मत को ज़िया सरसर को सबा बंदे को ख़ुदा क्या लिखना
हर शाम यहाँ शाम-ए-वीराँ आसेब-ज़दा रस्ते गलियाँ
जिस शहर की धुन में निकले थे वो शहर दिल-ए-बर्बाद कहाँ
सहरा को चमन बन कर गुलशन बादल को रिदा क्या लिखना
ज़ुल्मत को ज़िया सरसर को सबा बंदे को ख़ुदा क्या लिखना
ऐ मेरे वतन के फ़नकारो ज़ुल्मत पे न अपना फ़न वारो
ये महल-सराओं के बासी क़ातिल हैं सभी अपने यारो
विर्से में हमें ये ग़म है मिला इस ग़म को नया क्या लिखना
ज़ुल्मत को ज़िया सरसर को सबा बंदे को ख़ुदा क्या लिखना[17]

[Calamity stricken in every home, Suffocating is the air inside my home, Because of the misdeeds of an individual, Our motherland is being ridiculed by the world! How can I utter words of praise for such a devil human manifestation? How can I call the dark night the dawn? How can I call the toxic fumes the morning breeze? How can I refer to humans as GOD? Speak the truth, and you will be flogged (beaten) and imprisoned, This life is caught in the grip of lies, Human beings are cowering

---

[17] Lyrics available from https://www.rekhta.org/nazms/zulmat-ko-ziyaa-sarsar-ko-sabaa-bande-ko-khudaa-kyaa-likhnaa-zulmat-ko-ziyaa-sarsar-ko-sabaa-bande-ko-khudaa-kyaa-likhnaa-habib-jalib-nazms [Accessed 25.07.2023]

(crouch down in fear) in terror, While the blood-sucking monsters are on the rampage, How can this cruelty be called kindness? How can I write this disease as cure? How can I call the dark night the dawn? How can I call the toxic fumes the morning breeze? How can I refer to humans as GOD? Every evening here is one of desolation. Every road and alleyway was struck by calamity, With hope in our hearts we searched for a city, Where is that city now? Oh, my devastated heart? How can this desert be called a rose garden? How can I write of this cloud as a silver lining? How can I call the dark night the dawn? How can I call the toxic fumes the morning breeze? How can I refer to humans as GOD? Oh, fellow artists of my homeland! Don't sacrifice your art to the darkness, These people who live In palaces, All are murderers, oh my fellow companions! We have inherited this grief from the past, How can I write this grief as a new one? How can I call the dark night the dawn? How can I call the toxic fumes the morning breeze? How can I refer to humans as GOD?]18

Cultural activists have time and again evoked strong sentiments through their performances and have often been able to express complicated issues in simple language, one that is suited for the masses. Here again, one can take the example of Kalekuri Prasad, the Dalit poet from India, who tackled important issues pertaining to caste-based violence in India:

గాయాలు సలుపుతున్నా గుండెలమీద నీ పాదముద్రల్నే కదా మోశాను చావు ముంచుకొస్తున్నా నీతో బతుకునే కదా కోరుకున్నాను ప్రేమ కోసమే బతకలేకపోయినా కనీసం ప్రేమ కోసమే చద్దామనుకొన్నాను ప్రియా ! [...] సంగతేందిరా అని మీ వాళ్ళెవరన్నా అడిగితే నిన్ను ప్రేమించానని అరచి చెబుదామనుకున్నాను కాని నేను దొంగనని రచ్చబండ ఆరోపణ సాక్షివి నువ్వే కదా చచ్చిన శవాలను తగలబెట్టడం తెలుసు నాకు కాని బతికుండగానే మీ వాళ్ళు నాకు నిప్పు పెట్టారు ' తండ్రీ వీరేమి

---

18 Translation by Anish Adams. Available at: http://anish-adams.blogspot.com/2012/12/darkness-called-light.html [Accessed 27.07.2023]

చేయుచున్నారో వీరెరగరు కనుక వీరిని క్షమించుము '
పాదిరిగారు చెప్పిన ప్రభువు మాటలు గుర్తొస్తూనే ఉన్నాయి మనం గడిపిన
నిద్రలేని రాత్రులు సాక్షిగా
నీ కంట్లో ఒక్క కన్నీటి చుక్క మెరిసినా నిన్నూ నీ వాళ్ళనూ క్షమించేసే వాణ్ణి
గుండెల్లో నువ్వు రగిలించిన నిప్పుల కుంపటి వంటిమీద నీ
వాళ్ళంటించిన కిరసనాయిలు మంటలు ఏ బాధ ఎక్కువని అడిగితే
ఇప్పుడు చెప్పలేను ప్రియా!
ఈ మంటలు నన్ను అలుముకుంటుంటే
నువ్వు నన్ను వాటేసుకున్నట్టే వుంది|[19]

[I want to live with you, even if I am suffering from wounds, I want to live with you, even if I cannot live for love, at least I want to die for love, my dear. If any of your people asked me what was going on, I thought I would shout and say that I loved you, but you are a witness that they accused me of theft. They set me on fire 'God forgive them for they do not know what they are doing'. The words of the Lord spoken by the respected Padre are still remembered as the witness of the sleepless nights we spent. Even if a single drop of tear shines in your eye, I forgive you and your family, but you are like an ember of the fire that has kindled in the heart. If you ask what the most painful fire of the candles they set, I can't tell you! If these fires are burning me, now you have me!][20]

This poem from Prasad categorically attacks the ideological formulations that justify social evils such as honour killings that are caused mainly by caste hatred in the country phenomena of honor killings in India caused mainly by caste hatred in the country.[21] The language used in these two poems from poets from two very different spatialities and temporalities proves that

---

[19] Lyrics available from https://wirally.com/poem-by-revolutionary-telugu-poet-kalekuri-prasad-just-breaks-your-heart/ [Accessed 26.07.2023]
[20] Translation by Rajkumar Paseddula and the Author.
[21] See https://www.outlookindia.com/national/rising-honour-killings-in-india-a-look-at-5-brutal-murders-in-recent-past-news-296381# [Accessed 25.07.2023]

cultural activists often find it easier to express the burning issues of the day than traditional academics or political commentators. How anybody expresses their interpretation of the social reality around them is informed by the social conditioning that they have been made to live through.[22] In a society ridden with caste differences, illiteracy, and sexual violence, cultural modes of expression are immensely important. In societies such as India, where feudalism and capitalism have for decades co-existed with each other, the cultural mode of organizational politics often becomes the only mode of political transformation in the society because it is only through modes of cultural expression that socio-political ideas can reach most of the people in the country.

> How do you expect that a country with around 70% literacy, that too takes full cognizance that literacy in our country is defined differently and takes just the bare minimum qualifications or eligibility that a person has? Under these circumstances, you have to speak in the language that they understand and fortunately or unfortunately the political bloc has often failed to do so which has allowed us to function in the space. Our usage of folk songs and instruments stems from that. Their languages are simple, straightforward and easy to understand.

The activist here mentions how cultural forms of resistance use traditional folk models to speak about contemporary forms of exploitation. One can take the example of familial structures to further substantiate this point. The relationship that capitalism shares with traditions in societies such as India is the focal point of the social contradictions under contemporary capitalism in

---

[22] Berger, A. A. *Cultural Criticism: A Primer of Key Concepts*. Thousand Oaks, 1995.

India.[23] Employment plays a key role in mediating this relationship, especially in the case of women because women 'who [go to work in the factories] experience shifts in familial status as working-class households, governed by gender and age hierarchies favoring men and older people confront the reality of wage-earning young women. The factory job makes a young, unmarried feel—once the most disregarded member of her household—the major breadwinner'.[24] Under neoliberalism, the feminization of the workforce is a common occurrence. The student movements have been affected by these changes because such changes affect the class and gender composition on campuses, which then go on to affect the activism that emanates from campuses.

> The nature of the students' movement changes with the changes in the social structures. When neoliberalism was introduced, it changed the general contours of the student movement because it changed the aspirations of the students. It changed how students felt about their education and about their lives. (Student Activist, Delhi)

> Today we are getting a lot of students who come from families where both their parents are working. Twenty years ago being a housewife was a common sight for them. Today it has changed. This is progress no doubt but at the same time, it is also a major issue as far as certain issues are concerned. Some years ago we needed to only mainly talk about women's exploitation in the household, today we need to talk about social reproduction and its relevance. (Student Activist, Bengaluru)

---

[23] Lessinger, J. '"Love" in the Shadow of the Sewing Machine: A Study of Marriage in the Garment Industry of Chennai, South India'. In R. Kaur, & R. Palriwala (eds.), *Marrying in South Asia: Shifting Concepts, Changing Practices in a Globalising World*. Hyderabad: Orient Blackswan, 2014; Philips, A. 'Marriage, Women and Work: The Estate Tamils in Sri Lanka's Tea Plantations'. In R. Kaur, & R. Palriwala (eds.), *Marrying in South Asia: Shifting Concepts, Changing Practices in a Globalising World*. Hyderabad: Orient Blackswan, 2014.

[24] Lessinger ibid., p. 235.

The change in the general composition and socio-economic backgrounds of the student populace within the campus has a profound influence on the processes in which the student politics and movements function within the space. It changes the way students look at society because these changes have a critical effect on their self-reflection which is often critical to the generation of their consciousness about themselves and about society.[25] Any change in the broader contours of society changes the character of both the student and cultural movement of the country. This is because such changes in society not only alter the social space but also the constituent elements of the social space—both of which are critical to the development of a framework for cultural resistance.

---

[25] Adorno, T. W. *Negative Dialectics*. London: Routledge, 1973.

3
The Questioning of Modernity

गाव छोडब नही, जंगल छोडब नही, माय माटी छोडब नही लडाय छोडब नही।
बाँध बनाए, गाँव डुबोए, कारखाना बनाए, जंगल काटे, खदान खोदे, सेंक्चुरी बनाए,
जल जंगल जमीन छोडी हमिन कहा कहा जाए, विकास के भगवान बता हम कैसे जान बचाए॥
जमुना सुखी, नर्मदा सुखी, सुखी सुवर्णरेखा, गंगा बनी गन्दी नाली, कृष्णा काली रेखा,
तुम पियोगे पेप्सी कोला, बिस्लरी का पानी, हम कैसे अपना प्यास बुझाए, पीकर कचरा पानी?
पुरखे थे क्या मूरख जो वे जंगल को बचाए, धरती रखी हरी भरी नदी मधु बहाए,
तेरी हवसमें जल गई धरती, लुट गई हरियाली, मचली मर गई, पंछी उड गई जाने किस दिशाए॥
मंत्री बने कम्पनी के दलाल हम से जमीन छीनी, उनको बचाने लेकर आए साथ में पल्टनी
हो... अफसर बने है राजा ठेकेदार बने धनी, गाँव हमारी बन गई है उनकी कोलोनी ॥
बिरसा पुकारे एकजुट होवो छोडो ये खामोशी, मछवारे आवो, दलित आवो, आवो आदिवासी,
हो खेत खालीहान से जागो नगाडा बजाओ, लडाई छोडी चारा नही सुनो देस वासी ॥

— Bhagwaan Maaji[1]

[We will leave our village, we will not leave the jungle, we will not leave our soil, we will not leave our struggles. They come and build dams, drown our villages, build factories, cut forests, dig mines, and build sanctuaries. Leaving our water, forest and land where will we go? O' the God of Development, please tell us where should we go. The Ganga River is now dry, the same is the Narmada River, and the same is the Subarnarekha River. The Ganga has become a dirty drain, and the Krishna River is now like a black ray. You will Pepsi Cola and Bisleri[2] water, but how can we quench our thirst by drinking such garbage

---
[1] Lyrics from https://livingsimply938206083.wordpress.com/2018/10/12/gaon-chodab-nahi-protest-song/ [Accessed on 08.08.2023]
[2] A popular brand that sells packaged drinking water in India.

water? Were our forefathers foolish that they saved the forest, kept the earth green, and the river flowing with honey? The earth has been burnt by your lust for power and money, and the greenery has been looted. The fishes have died and the birds have flown away. The ministers have become brokers for the companies and snatched all our land from us. To do this, they brought soldiers with them. The officers have become kings, and the contractors have become rich, our village has become their colony. Birsa Munda, our great leader, has given a call to arms to break this silence. Come all the fishermen, come all the Dalits, come all the tribal people. Wake up from your fields and play your drums. All my country people, there is no choice left but to fight][3]

The problems that plague India the most are intertwined with multiple issues encompassing dimensions of caste hierarchy and power, educational backwardness, the disintegration of traditional familial structures, etc., most of which have been affected by the capitalist mode of development.[4] One of the pioneering Marxist sociologists from India, Akshay Ramanlal Desai had written, 'To discern a change in a system, to recognize its direction, to understand the subjective and objective forces which bring it about and further to consciously accelerate the process of change by helping the progressive trends within the changing system—this constitutes a scientific approach to and active creative intervention in the life of a system'.[5] Cultural activists have always been widely affected by the changing social and political landscape around them that Desai spoke about. Within the aegis of the student struggles, questions surrounding such changes have been important ones, because student movements themselves are characterized by a certain dynamic nature that is often unheard of in mainstream politics, they

---

[3] Translation by author.

[4] Desai, A. R. 'Sociological Analysis of India'. In A. R. Desai (ed), *Rural Sociology in India*. Bombay: Popular Prakashan, 1969.

[5] Desai, A. R. 'Introduction'. In A. R. Desai (ed), *Peasant Struggles in India*. New Delhi: Oxford University Press, 1979, pp. 17-18.

naturally get more affected by these changes. Most of these changes have an intimate relationship with the idea of modernity that a society possesses, which in turn is related to aspects such as gender equality, freedom of expression, etc. Modernity has always occupied an important position in the realm of culture and cultural studies. Culture has been viewed as something that often has the power to push society towards modernization in a socialist sense. The artists and performers have an important role to play in this regard. Faiz Ahmed Faiz had written in the 1950s:

> Who are we? We the writers, poets, artists and what can we contribute, if anything to avert the mortal calamities threatening mankind? We are the offspring, in the direct line of descent of the music makers of old. In times gone by, these ancient ancestors of ours, could make the rain come down with their songs, they could make the deserts bloom. And they not only implicitly believed that they had these powers, their community believed it too. This is because they found the dreams and longings, words and music that the people could not find for themselves.[6]

Faiz is speaking about the important role that cultural activists and practitioners can play in the construction of a modern egalitarian society. There has always been an intrinsic relationship between culture and the progressive idea of modernity. This is manifested through the fact that issues such as the oppression of women and Dalits—issues that are often caused by the masses' belief in heretical norms—have always found a more powerful voice within the aegis of cultural struggle than they have within mainstream political discourse. This is partly because of the failure of contemporary political discourse to provide adequate voices to such sections of the populace and also partly because of the historical role that non-political actors have played in the

---

[6] Faiz, F. A. The Role of the Artist. There are almost no versions of the essay available in English in India. The one that has been reproduced above has been extracted from the website of a NGO, *The Miraculuous Love Kids*. Available at: https://miraculouslovekids.org/the-role-of-the-artist-faiz-ahmed-faiz/ [Accessed 25.07.2023]

context of India, especially in the context of local politics. While the state does exist as a formal institution, it does not exist as a practical body for them because their lifeworld is dominated and dictated by the informal arrangements managed and run by the dominant sections of the populace.[7] Cultural modes of expressing dissatisfaction and dissent often make it easier for such individuals to become one with the dissent they exhibit towards the system in place. Under the conditions created by contemporary capitalism, it is often the case that it is the upwardly mobile middle class that possesses, or rather reserves for itself, the most important aspects of the power of articulation by dint of its socio-economic and cultural capital.[8] Cultural modes of protest, in this scenario, often empower people coming from marginalized sections of society to voice their opinions on matters that would have otherwise remained outside the sphere of their influence.

The constant domination of an urban elite in the realm of politics has left most of the marginalized populace devoid of the critical voice that is required to make oneself heard in the kind of dehumanizing space constructed under neoliberal capitalism. The middle class in India came into being under the patronage of the British government and its roots 'lay not in industry or trade, [which were] increasingly controlled by [others], but in government service or the professions of law, education, journalism or medicine'.[9] The growth of the service sector has been a crucial factor in the development of the Indian middle class,[10] which has been an instrumental force in the creation of the social circumstances necessary for the decline of the welfare

---

[7] Harriss-White, B. 'Work and Wellbeing in Informal Economies: The Regulative Roles of Institutions of Identity and the State'. *World Development, 38*(2), 2010, 170-83.

[8] Le Grand, J., & Winter, D. 'The Middle Classes and the Welfare State under Conservative and Labour Governments'. *Journal of Public Policy, 6*(4), 1986, 399-430.

[9] Sarkar, S. *Modern India, 1885-1947*. London: Palgrave Macmillan, 1989, p. 68.

[10] Fernandes, L. *India's New Middle Class: Democratic Politics in an Era of Economic Reform*. Minneapolis: University of Minnesota Press, 2006; Dickey, S. *Living Class in Urban India*. Oxford: Oxford University Press, 2016.

state and the creation of the neoliberal society, which was in synchronization with the western bourgeois values, that the middle class adhered to in urban India.[11] The development of the middle class in India was characterized by its growing support for market-driven policies replacing the welfare state which has led:

> The post-Liberalisation period [to witness] the highest rise in the middle segment of the new middle-class households ... mainly from the professional and managerial white-collar job holders placed at the mid-level salary brackets, or [from] the business class, have considerable income, mostly [having] more than one earner, are conscious consumerists, and spend a part of their money on maintaining a lifestyle ... informed and influenced by advertisements and images of the glitterati.[12]

Being a member of the middle class in India is related to the ability to consume certain cultural and material commodities in a particular way that exhibits the cultural and social capital that an individual possesses such as 'formal educational qualifications and English language [proficiency which] have been defining characteristics of the new middle-class modernity in urban India'.[13] The middle class in urban areas within a liberalizing Indian Economy, schooled in accordance with bourgeois and petty-bourgeois values, becomes the perfect manifestation of the uncritical non-capitalist class that capitalism desires to create in

---

[11] Chakrabarti, D. 'D. P. Mukherji and the Middle Class in India'. *Sociological Bulletin,* 59(2), 2010, 235-55; Chattopadhyay, S. *Being English: Indian Middle Class and the Desire for Anglicisation.* Abingdon: Routledge, 2022.

[12] Jha, M. K., & Pushpendra. 'Contextualising India's New Middle Class: Intersectionalities and Social Mobility'. In M. K. Jha & Pushpendra (eds.), *Beyond Consumption: India's New Middle Class in the Neo-Liberal State.* New Delhi: Routledge, 2022, p. 4.

[13] Ganguly, S. 'In the Pursuit of Middle-Classness: Exploring the Aspirations and Strategies of the Urban Poor in Neoliberal Delhi'. In M. K. Jha & Pushpendra (eds.), *Beyond Consumption: India's New Middle Class in the Neo-Liberal State.* New Delhi: Routledge, 2022, p. 98.

society.[14] The domination of such values, which often rest upon factors such as a subjective sense of being 'English' in India enabled the upwardly mobile class and the individuals therein to imitate the mores and social norms of the British which helped them to explore their own modern selves within a conflicting relationship with the broader social reality and society in general.[15] In other words, these value structures helped them articulate their own selves as an exceptional element within the social structure, very different from the waged working class. The domination that the middle class waged over the socio-cultural life of the nation also influenced the kind of choices that people make concerning the kind of culture they practice, and consume and the mode in which they do the same.[16] An activist recollected:

> For the longest period of time, the only English song that I could sing was This Land is My Land by Woody Guthrie. When I first started singing the song, I did not know who had sung it or whose composition it was, but I still continued to sing it. It empowered me. 'This land is our land' was my introduction to the English language basically. Today I am a professional sound engineer, I guess this owes a lot to the song. (Student Cultural Activist, Nagaland)

The activist further narrated how the song had almost become a status symbol for him while he was growing up in the 1990s in India, among his friends and peers. Such influence of singers and performers from the West was not an entirely new aspect of the cultural movement Even before singers such as Seeger and Guthrie, the early influences on the progressive cultural movement in India were Russian plays and songs, one of the

---

[14] Althusser, L. *On the Reproduction of Capitalism: Ideology and Ideological State Apparatuses.* London: Verso, 2014.

[15] Chattopadhyay op cit.

[16] Bryson, B. 'Symbolic Exclusion and Musical Dislikes'. In L. Spillman (ed), *Cultural Sociology.* London: Blackwell, 2002; Hunt, D. 'Raced Ways of Seeing'. In L. Spillman (ed), *Cultural Sociology.* London: Blackwell, 2002.

most notable ones among which was Maxim Gorky's Mother which was staged in Calcutta in 1953.[17] The relationship with Russian literature, songs and plays was such that even today many Russian books and pamphlets are considered to be essential readings within many socio-political circles. Introducing a recent volume that speaks about these issues, Vijay Prashad writes, 'Generations in the Global South grew up with Soviet books on our shelves. If we could afford books, they would be lavishly illustrated Soviet Children's books, then a volume or two of Tolstoy and then, finally, perhaps a few volumes of Lenin's writings.[18] Soviet literature and culture have played a tremendous role in shaping how the Indian society, or at least a particular generation, imagined a better future.[19]

The progressive cultural movement has since its inception been conversant with the idea of initiating discussion and debates in a vibrant and democratic manner within the organization.[20] The progressive cultural organizations had since the onset understood the importance of internal democracy within their organization. Many activists who have been working with the cultural fronts noted that their visions surrounding the democratic revolution in India were based on an opposition to all varieties of chauvinism because any kind of chauvinism leads to the death knell of all forms of art in the society, as had been put forward by the iconic Balraj Sahni—one of the most talented actors that India has ever produced and who remained one of the most prolific proponents of the progressive cultural movement of the country—in a speech delivered in Assam, a tiny north-eastern

---

[17] Biswas, H. (1953/2017). Gorky's Mother on Calcutta Stage. In S. Pradhan (ed.), *Marxist Cultural Movement in India Volume 2: Chronicles and Documents (1947-1958)*. Kolkata: National Book Agency.

[18] Prasad, Vijay. 'Introduction'. In *The East was Read*, edited by Vijay Prashad. New Delhi: Leftword, 2019, p. 13.

[19] Djagalov, R. 'Progress Publishers: A Short History'. In V. Prashad (ed), *The East was Read: Socialist Culture in the Third World*. New Delhi: Leftword, 2019; Mishra op cit.

[20] Unity. 'Organisational Principles'. In *Marxist Cultural Movement in India Volume 2: Chronicles and Documents (1947-1958)*, edited by Sudhi Pradhan. Kolkata: National Book Agency, 1953; Deshpande, S. Halla Bol: The Death and Life of Safdar Hashmi. New Delhi: Leftword, 2020.

state of India in the 1950s itself.[21] Cultural groups such as the IPTA in the country have been instrumental forces in the rendering mainstream of numerous folk traditions in the country in combination with classical and modern musical traditions that often entail within themselves the usage of tunes and instruments considered to be unsuitable for contemporary mainstream music and cultural performances.[22] Take the example of the dafli,[23] an instrument that has largely been relegated to obscurity but kept alive by musicians of resistance:

> We make it a point to use instruments that are easily accessible to the common masses. That is the reason we do not use drums or other such expensive instruments. We have even restricted the use of harmonium in our plays because the cost of that has gone up, the same goes for things such as guitar or dholaks. The most common element in our performances now is the dafli, it is easily recognizable, gives a good sound and more importantly is accessible to most. (Cultural Activist, Delhi)

Organizations such as the IPTA and PWM were instrumental in bringing out such folk instruments and traditions of the social context in which it conducted its plays through such a process.[24] The relationship between the folk and modern forms of art is one of the basic fulcrums around which the cultural movement of the country has been founded. It has worked in tandem with both the traditions working towards the creation of a unique Indian modernism that does not devalue either its traditions or its drive for modernity as understood in a Western sense. The

---

[21] Sahni, Balraj. 'Inaugural Speech to the Third Assam IPTA State Conference'. In *Marxist Cultural Movement in India Volume 2: Chronicles and Documents (1947-1958)*, edited by Sudhi Pradhan. Kolkata: National Book Agency, 1955.

[22] Damodaran, S. 'People's Music: The Musical Repertoire of the Indian Peoples' Theatre Association'. In *The Progressive Cultural Movement: A Critical History*. New Delhi: SAHMAT, 2017.

[23] A 'dafli' is an instrument that is similar to a hand-held drum.

[24] Unity, op cit.

relationship between culture and politics in the subcontinent is a deep and intimate one and transcends the standard patterns set in the West. Considering India, it is important to take into consideration that studies about it have often been plagued by value bias and a certain amount of ideological intonation because the Global North has been accepted as a standardized paradigm, which has often not taken into its fold ideas surrounding progress and modernity in countries such as India.[25] Such concepts cannot be one-dimensional ones when they are sought to be implemented in the context of India because local processes have always played an important role in the way in which ideas surrounding the same have been formed with many ideological and political processes getting dictated by social rather than legal structures.[26]

The idea of progress that is dominant within contemporary society is an idea dictated by how one conceptualizes urbanism and its relationship to modernity, one that often does not pay adequate attention to the local and dialectical processes.[27] This is where cultural activism becomes extremely important in countries like India. The cultural movement in India has progressed in regions even where economic development and social integration with the mainstream society have been slow and stunted such as the cultural movement in Dandakaranya[28] led by the Jana Natya Mandali (JNM). One of the major advantages of the cultural movement is that it has been able to work through the numerous indigenous linguistic and cultural traditions of the country. Chetna has written in detail on the

---

[25] Desai, A. R. 'Need for Revaluation of a Concept'. In A. R. Desai (ed), *Essays on Modernization of Underdeveloped Societies: Volume 1*. New York: Humanities Press, 1972; Omvedt op cit.

[26] Harriss-White, B. *India Working: Essays on Society and Economy*. London: Cambridge University Press, 2003.

[27] Champagne, D. 'Explaining the Capitalist City: An Idea of Progress in Harvey's Marxism'. *Theory and Society, 47*, 2018, 717-35.

[28] One of the most prominent centres of the Maoist Movement in India. For more details, see https://theprint.in/pageturner/excerpt/the-idea-of-dandakaranya-as-a-breeding-zone-of-maoists-took-birth-at-a-dinner-table/1245332/ [Accessed 09.08.2023]

ways in which the revolutionary cultural movement has enabled the sustenance of the indigenous cultures and languages in the hinterlands of India through the usage of the language and the folk traditions in various songs, plays and other cultural forms—and especially through the manner in which they have integrated the cultural forms of the protest with the material oppression faced by the poorest of the poor,[29] through songs and poems such as:

> Mutti hettad sangeru mantha, Netral Janda Olsure Mantha
> Netral Janda Olsure Mantha, Bhoomithe Pura Netral Podthasi
> Garib Thoreki Saayitha Manneke

[Having Hammer, Sickle in it, Red Flag is Flying High; Red Flag is Flying High, Becoming Red Symbol in the Sky; Supporting the Oppressed People][30]

Cultural resistance allows the left-wing and progressive forces to contextualize their theoretical foundations into the most subtle domain of human lives. It allows the marginalized and exploited individuals to imagine freedom elevating themselves from the exclusionary and exploitative social circumstances within which they must live their lives[31]. Cultural resistance when combined with the youthful energy of the students' movement provides liberation movements with the much-needed liberatory imagination.

---

[29] Chetna, N. M. *Three Decades of Dandakaranya Literary and Cultural Movement 1980-2010: People's War is the Refrain of the Song.* Kolkata: SETU, 2017.

[30] Song composed by JNM, quoted from Chetna op cit., pp. 37-38.

[31] The Freedom Theatre School Alumni. A Conversation about Cultural Resistance. Interview Compiled by J. Wallin, J. Stanczak & O. Johansson. In O. Johansson & J. Wallin (eds.), *The Freedom Theatre*. New Delhi: Leftword, 2018.

4
Dangers of Cultural Resistance under Hindutva

बोल के लब आज़ाद हैं तेरे बोल ज़बां अब तक तेरी है
तेरा सुतवां जिस्म है तेरा बोल के जान अब तक तेरी है
देख के अहंगर की दुकान में तुंद है शोले, सुर्ख है अहां
खुल्ने लागे क्चफ्लोन के दहाने फैला हर एक ज़ंजीर का दामन
बोल ये थोड़ा वक्त बहुत है जिस्म-ओ ज़बान की मौत से पहले
बोल के सच ज़िंदा है अब तक बोल जो कुछ कहना है, कह ले!

[Speak, for your lips are still free, Speak, for your tongue is still yours, Your body, though frail, is still yours, Speak, for your life is still yours. Look, in the blacksmith's workshop, The flames are hot, the steel is red, The mouths of the locks are beginning to open, The links of chains are coming undone. Speak, for the little time you have is enough. Before your body and tongue die. Speak, for truth still lives. Speak up, say that which you must!]

Faiz Ahmed Faiz[1]

Munshi Premchand, one of the most celebrated Indian writers, wrote these lines during the 1930s:

> ... our literary taste is undergoing a rapid transformation. It is coming more and more to grip with the realities of life; it interests itself with society or man as a social unit. It is not satisfied now with the singing of frustrated love; or with writing to satisfy only our sense of wonder; it concerns itself with the problems of our life; and

---

[1] Mir & Mir op cit., p. 23.

such themes have a social value. The literature which does not arouse in us a critical spirit, or satisfy our spiritual and intellectual needs, which is not "force-giving" and dynamic, which does not awaken our sense of beauty, which does not make us face the grim realities of life in a spirit of determination, has no use for us today. It cannot even be termed as literature.[2]

There are various cultural forms that have emerged to counter the fears of Premchand, and later also of personalities such as Adorno and Marcuse. Progressive bands such as Laal from Pakistan and Majma from India have been attempting to rediscover such realist cultural forms of expression that shaped the freedom struggle and the struggle for social justice after independence in the Indian subcontinent—that includes all the three, India, Pakistan, and Bangladesh. Through their renditions of popular poets and singers, they have been trying to generate an alternative socio-political discourse in South Asia that counters the cultural nationalism that has gripped the subcontinent characterized by communal attacks on minorities across the region.[3] Any form of cultural resistance is a product of the contradictions of the social scenario within which it takes root, which plays a critical role in its formation as well as the political and social undertones that characterize it. These complexities, in the case of organizations such as the IPTA and JANAM greatly influenced the kind of music, techniques, and words that they used in their performances.[4]

The usage of simpler languages and the creation of a popular form make it easier for them to focus on issues that within the domain of mainstream politics often remain plagued by political jargon and a form of rationalization that only used them for political gains. The language that political cultural activism uses

---

[2] Premchand, M. 'The Nature and Purpose of Literature'. In S. Pradhan (ed.), *Marxist Cultural Movement in India, Volume 1: Chronicles and Documents (1936-1947)*. Kolkata: National Book Agency, 1936/2017, p. 79.

[3] Menon op cit.; Jha, D. K. *Shadow Armies: Fringe Organisations and Foot soldiers of Hindutva*. New Delhi: Juggernaut Books, 2017.

[4] Damodaran op cit.; Ghosh op cit., Jalil 2020 op cit.

is one that is laden with socio-political metaphors capable of inspiring people,[5] which becomes critical under neo-fascist regimes such as the one in India which do not speak kindly to forms of art because art exposes the most subtle contradictions of the society in a language that can be easily accessed by almost everybody in the society. That constitutes the basic ideas behind the creation of a cultural front against the onslaught of capitalism. Because of this unique quality that progressive culture possesses. Marcuse noted in 1969:

> The thesis of the end of art has become a familiar slogan; radicals take it as a truism; they reject or 'suspend' art as part of bourgeois culture, just as they reject or suspend its literature or philosophy. This verdict extends easily to all theory, all intelligence (no matter how 'creative') that does not spark action and practice, that does not noticeably help to change the world, that does not … break through the universe of mental and physical pollution in which we live.[6]

Marcuse here is speaking in similar terms as Munshi Premchand —who preceded him in analyzing this quality of progressive art by a gap of more than 35 years. The historic role that progressive art has possessed in making the people aware of the oppression that they face and its quality—often unexplored—to make them organize for the same has made progressive cultural organizations a central issue for the State, as far as its desire to ensure law and order is concerned. In the past, the state often took a more nuanced approach towards cultural organizations because it saw such organizations as being reformist—which they were because their primary target was the betterment of the cultural life of the people—in nature without having much of an impact on the political fabric of the country. In other words, the

---

[5] Ghosh, A. *A History of the Jana Natya Manch: Plays for the People*. New Delhi: SAGE, 2012.

[6] Marcuse, H. 'Art as a Form of Reality'. In D. Kellner (ed.), Collected Papers of Herbert Marcuse: Volume 4: Art and Liberation. London: Routledge, 1969/2007, p. 140.

state understood the differences between progressive and revolutionary[7] and acted following classical liberal values—promoting reformism to subdue any kind of revolutionism from creeping up to keep the general structure of the society unchanged and in favor of the status quo. Cultural modes of expressing dissent are related to policy decisions that influence the State's position on certain modes of cultural expressions and artifacts and require a more nuanced approach to the same, especially concerning how ideology and hegemony work in society and representational mediums.[8] Of late, the cultural movement and the activists associated with it have faced an innumerable number of attacks on themselves, not only because of their political leanings but also because of the kind of content that they communicate through their songs. The attacks on cultural activists prove that the nature of the state in India has undergone a tremendous shift gradually moving rightwards, and as one student cultural activist put it:

> India under the BJP is a changed country from the one that I grew up in. Previously yes, Congress also attacked. It was not that they were saints. But there was still a decorum. Democratic and progressive voices were still shut down. Take the example of Comrade Safdar Hashmi, who was killed by Congress goons. The BJP is no better, see what is happening to Varavara Rao, see what is happening to Kabir Kala Manch. The situation is the same for us, the problem is that while the Congress could at least talk sense and secularism, the BJP has none of it. (Senior Cultural Activist, Delhi)

Numerous cultural activists such as Sheetal Sathe of the Kabir Kala Manch and the acclaimed radical poet, Varavara Rao (aged 82!) have been arrested and jailed on various grounds under the

---

[7] Ali op cit.

[8] Bennett, T. 'Putting Policy into Cultural Studies'. In J. Storey (ed), *What is Cultural Studies: A Reader*. London: Arnold, 1997.

BJP government.[9] Under the BJP government that is at the helm of affairs in India, there has come into being a grave risk even in organizing cultural fronts, because cultural fronts—due to them functioning directly within the public sphere—often come in direct contact with hostile far-right groups in the civil society in addition to the government in place as well. This has become a major hindrance in the pathways of the organized left, or the left in general, because cultural activism in contemporary times has been one of the major aspects of the struggle that the left and the progressive organizations and individuals have been engaged in against the inherent feudalism in the Indian society that has intensified under the aegis of contemporary neoliberal Hindutva.[10] It has been an instrumental force in evoking contradictions that otherwise would not have been addressed appropriately by the forces of the State including issues such as caste discrimination, female infanticide, etc. In other words, in many ways, forms of cultural activism have done what the state should ideally have done in a society such as India. This includes making the citizens aware of global culture, bringing forth important issues pertaining to constructing an egalitarian society, making caste atrocities visible, and the like. These issues were focused upon by some of the activists interviewed:

> In India, the state has failed many of us. It has failed to provide most of the citizens with adequate education, and health in addition to its problems about hunger, shelter, etc. As a result, most of the population has remained trapped in a pre-modern form of existence. Their sense of life has mostly been restricted to sustenance. Amidst that kind of a situation, the kind of cultural performance that we do gives them some form of respite. We provide them with a sense of cultural upliftment, ideally, the state should have done that. A civilization is not built by money and economics alone. (Senior Cultural Activist, Delhi)

---

[9] See https://thewire.in/rights/kabir-kala-manch-members-bail-sc ; https://www.bbc.com/news/world-asia-india-62488187 [Accessed 25.07.2023]
[10] Teltumbde, A. *The Republic of Caste*. New Delhi: Navayana, 2018.

> Cultural activism is an extremely important terrain as far as India is concerned, especially in the context of Dalits. Dalits still lack the language of articulation. On most campuses, most of them have no idea how to go about their everyday lives. This stems from the historic exploitation that has been meted out to them, often muting them. Cultural activism makes them speak out because there they can just go unleashed without caring much about the kind of language and aesthetics used. (Student Activist, Bengaluru)

Cultural activism in such situations produces certain radical ways of knowing society. The importance that cultural activists exhibit points toward the vitality of cognitive justice within student movements and society in general.[11] Cultural activism in countries such as India are not merely forms of activism, they are rather ways in which the society witnesses the world. How a certain Faiz Ahmed Faiz or a certain Bishnu Prasad Rabha or a Gorakh Pandey or a Kalekuri Prasad sees the world becomes the lens through which countless others view, interpret, and analyze their social reality and the world. These figures provided the much-needed framework to millions of people through which they can escape the utter hopelessness that comes to characterize their lives under capitalism. The ability to articulate is one of the major obstacles that many individuals face in their everyday struggles in countries such as India where the general consciousness of the masses has remained at a level, or has been made to remain at a level, where despite being affected by the growing inequalities of the society, they continue to appreciate the existent state of affairs constituting a one-dimensional society where they are left without much individual or communitarian agency and hope for a better life.[12] Cultural activism helps marginalized communities in the process of articulating their own oppression in a language that is their own—without delving

---

[11] Dawson, M. C. 'Student Activism against the Neocolonial University: Exploring a Sociology of Absences, Emergences, and Hidden Fires'. *Counterfutures*, 4, 2017. DOI: https://doi.org/10.26686/cf.v4i0.6405

[12] Marcuse, 1964, op cit.

into the academic or political jargon that usually characterizes television narratives or university-based discourses.

The songs and plays that such expressions embody often run antithetically to the dominant narratives and established norms in society. Such modes of expression act as a bridge between mainstream and modern forms of art and the radical arts and culture prevalent within society. Radical art is simultaneously artistic and political which is created with a goal of liberation and against the oppressive tendencies prevalent in the society. Cultural resistance enables the politicization of the everyday life of the people.[13] Since culture is often seen as something that transcends human boundaries more easily than other forms of political articulation. It can provide future pathways to students and people coming from marginalized backgrounds in ways that mainstream political activism cannot, as an activist states:

> My time with the cultural group at the university actually prepared the ground for what I am today. It gave me confidence you know, coming from a marginalized background, both socially and financially, I was not confident enough to speak in public. The rehearsals and performances helped me gain enough confidence through which I could gather the courage to speak up, and sometimes, merely speaking up itself is a revolutionary act. (Former Student Activist, Hyderabad)

The activist mentioned here comes from a highly marginalized caste in rural Andhra Pradesh, one which has probably seen only a handful of its members leaving the boundaries of their ancestral lives, both economically and culturally. Cultural activism constitutes one of the most vibrant resistances towards the dominant forces of homogenization that characterize capitalism in the 21st century. Even among those coming from the middle classes in India, engagement with cultural organizations often proves to be beneficial to them as individuals:

---

[13] Bhattacharya, M. (2017). Moment and Movement: Creativity in the Cause of the People. In *The Progressive Cultural Movement: A Critical History*. New Delhi: SAHMAT.

> I come from an upper-middle-class background, but even then, I was suffering from problems of self-confidence. My association with the singing group actually helped me resolve much of that. While being part of the troupe, you sing in the open, it is different than how you do that in a school or a college. It is actually a very good tool for personality development. (Former Student Activist, Assam)

In other words, forms of cultural activism play a tremendous role in the shaping of social identities in contemporary society. This remains in synchronization with the fact that political theatre, or for that matter, all forms of cultural resistance-based activities are major contributions to:

> ... a definition, a revaluation of the cultural identity of a people or a section of society ... [and] can, by allowing [threatened communities] to speak, help them to survive ... [and at the same time,] it can mount an attack on the standardization of culture and consciousness which is a function of late industrial/early technological 'consumerist' societies everywhere ... [and] often is linked to a wider political struggle for the right of a people or a section of a society to control its own destiny.[14]

The culture of a particular society is the key to understanding the soul of the society. It is the key to understanding the complexity and diversity that characterize societies and produce a combination of economic determinants and social relations that guide the cultural fabric.[15] Because of the unique nature of socio-political and cultural contradictions that India presents, it becomes critical for any work engaging with social change in India to define what it means by 'social change' at the outset. While quantitative change engages with statistics, 'Social change is qualitative change if it establishes essentially different forms of

---

[14] McGrath, John. *The Bone won't Break: On Theatre and Hope in Hard Times.* London: Methuen, 1990, p. 142.
[15] Williams, R. *Culture and Society.* London: Hogarth Press, 1987.

human existence, with a new social division of labor, new modes of control over the productive process, a new morality, etc.'.[16] The question that looms large at this point is whether traditional socio-political organizations have formulated an alternative narrative of history and developmental socio-political theory in India that adequately addresses the issues concerned with such qualitative changes. Numerous social and political groups have been formed in India to pursue an egalitarian model of social development focused on qualitative transformation, and most of them have taken the aspect of cultural transformation very seriously.

Cultural activism makes it possible for the progressive forces to comment on the most mundane events of everyday life so much so that when the IPTA used to do it quite effectively, its sphere of influence extended even to the mainstream section of the Hindi film industry with many celebrities visiting their centers and engaging with them.[17] Student movements also have this innate capacity to attract figures holding important positions in society because of the youthful zeal and spirit that they embody within themselves, which often become extremely important because they at times perform a role that cannot be performed or even envisaged by commercial or political agents.[18] Such a revolutionary and mass nature of progressive cultural activism makes it an entity to be feared by the far-right in the context of India—more so when it emanates from students and echoes through their movements against social justice.

Issues of gender, caste and ethnicity-based discrimination are much more effectively invoked within cultural narratives within the campuses than the politics that student groups within campuses engage in. Cultural politics provides a critical platform

---

[16] Marcuse, H. 'The Problem of Social Change in a Technological Society'. In D. Kellner (ed), *Collected Papers of Herbert Marcuse: Volume 2*. London: Routledge, 1961/2001, p. 38.

[17] Sahni, K., & Joshi, P. C. *Balraj and Bhisham Sahni: Brothers in Political Theatre*. New Delhi: SAHMAT, 2012; Jalil, R. 'The Glory Days of the Progressive Writers' Movement'. In *The Progressive Cultural Movement: A Critical History*. New Delhi: SAHMAT, 2017.

[18] Hall, S., & Whannel, P. *The Popular Arts*. London: Hutchinson, 1964.

to progressive politics for delving into issues that are at times considered to be 'closed-door' issues even within the liberal-minded campuses of the country which include issues such as menstrual health, caste-based discrimination, and the like. This becomes possible because culture is an all-encompassing field of analysis with aspects such as hegemonic domination and ideological superimposition becoming parts of the overall and broad cultural traits that the nation and the society possess. Because of its all-encompassing nature political formations from the left to the right have realized the importance that they need to according the cultural struggle in their respective political strategies towards bringing forward not only an analytical discourse in the society but also establishing a popular perception in favor of their ideas of social justice or social injustice.

5
Cultural Struggles and the Contradictions of India

> संपविला देह जरी संपणार नाही मती
> धर्माच्या गारदयांनो कशी रोखणार गती ...
>
> - Sachin Mali, Kabir Kala Manch, *Sampvila Deh Zari*[1]
> [Even if they kill the body, They cannot kill thought, O religious mercenaries Can you stop the wheel of progress?][2]

Progressive cultural personalities have often, since the beginning of the 1990s, 'conceptualize[d] the state as a "sinner" and have [had] no qualms being ruthless with their daily execution of politicians'.[3] Progressive art exposes the real situation of society. It is critical to the generation of anti-establishment sentiments in the society that can combine with the dissatisfactions that result from the economic exploitation in the society. For example, a recent article in The Hindu stated the importance that music had in the Indian struggle for freedom where singers and cultural activists converted anti-imperialist music into mainstream voices of protest playing a major role in the creation of a lifestyle based on resistance to the British Empire in India.[4] These songs played

---

[1] Full Lyrics available at https://samatechigani.blogspot.com/2017/03/blog-post_1.html [Accessed on 03.08.2023]

[2] Translation by Aarefa Johari. See https://scroll.in/article/948345/the-art-of-resistance-kabir-kala-manch-gives-us-a-timeless-song-of-defiance-in-times-of-fascism [Accessed on 03.08.2023]

[3] Menon, S. Cartoonists against Communalism. In *Punch Line*. New Delhi: SAHMAT, p. 6.

[4] V. S. 'How Music Played a Significant Role in the Freedom Struggle'. *The Hindu*, 2022, August 11.

a critical role in the generation of a sense of subjective liberation in colonial India. Politico-cultural activism has always played a key role in the context of India as has already been noted many times in the book. However, of late, the quality of such cultural activism has declined seriously, something which has gripped the attention of critical activists and thinkers, primarily because such activism draws directly from the left-progressive movement in the society which has declined considerably in India since the 1990s.[5] At this moment, it is critical to revisit the early progenitors of the progressive cultural movement in the country and their views surrounding what actually constructs progressive art. Munshi Premchand had written:

> For us 'progressive' is that which creates in us the power to act; which makes us examine those subjective and objective causes that have brought us to such a pass if sterility and degeneration; and finally, which helps us to overcome and remove those causes, and become [human] once again. We have no use ... for those poetical fancies which overwhelm us with their insistence on the ephemeral nature of this world and whose only effect is to fill our hearts with despondency and indifference.[6]

The broad definition of 'progressive' that Premchand identifies has contributed significantly to the generation of a discourse suited to appropriating international figures to the landscape of India. Such a definition has contributed not only to how radicals understand art but also to the entire process of understanding the politics associated with the word 'progressive'. Premchand's definition lays bare the relationship that exists between theory and praxis in the realm of cultural activism. It is this emphasis on

---

[5] Deshpande, G. '"Political Theatre has Decline"'. Interview by Moloyashree Hashmi. In S. Deshpande (ed), *Theatre of the Streets: The Jana Natya Manch Experience*. New Delhi: JANAM, 2013.

[6] Premchand, M. 'The Nature and Purpose of Literature'. In S. Pradhan (ed), *Marxist Cultural Movement in India: Chronicles and Documents (1936-1947): Volume 1*. Kolkata: National Book Agency, 1979/2017, pp. 79-80.

the concrete nature of the term that can enable one to understand the abstraction associated with terms such as 'internationalism' in cultural activism that has made national boundaries seem non-existent to cultural activists. Songs of revolutionary poets from Pakistan, such as Faiz Ahmed Faiz and Habib Jalib have been mainstays in the campus cultural politics in India for years now. Left-wing cultural groups have sung their songs, enacted plays based on their songs and have drawn their graffiti on the walls of institutions, making them public figures in India countering the right-wing narrative against Urdu and Urdu-speakers that tends to pain them as 'invaders' and 'aliens'. Cultural organizations have been examples of how songs can become articulations of arguments that are perhaps too difficult to be expressed in words. The cultural performances of these groups, which often occur at night often entitled 'Nights of Resistance' have grown to become important events in the revolutionary calendar of campuses across India. This chapter looks at the deep impact of these events on the overall social fabric on the campuses along with how cultural politics of a progressive nature can affect the political articulations of contemporary times.

Cultural struggles have often progressed in conjunction with their role in enabling the marginalized sections of gain education and obtain the ability to imagine a better future.[7] Modes of voicing one's dissent, tend to resolve the contradictions that exist between structure and agency in a neoliberal world.[8] The struggle between structure and agency is an important one because individuals are affected by the structural contradictions such as the power relations in place that determine and get determined by the agency that they enjoy in a particular context.[9] Most of these issues play out in the everyday lives of the actors involved, and the basic quality of any materialist

---

[7] Mally, L. *Culture of the Future: The Proletkult Movement in Revolutionary Russia.* Berkeley: The University of California Press, 1990.

[8] Banfield, Grant. *Critical Realism for Marxist Sociology of Education.* Abingdon: Routledge, 2016.

[9] Archer, M. S. *Culture and Agency: The Place of Culture in Social Theory.* Cambridge: Cambridge University Press, 1996.

philosophy worth its salt is to be able to explain the nuanced issues presented by the everyday contradictions that human beings face. As Debiprasad Chattopadhyaya wrote:

> Human beings have won over the world. But in what sense? How? Is it in the same vein as the colonial forces won over the [lands and bodies of] indigenous people? The colonisers won over the land and implemented their norms and laws upon those lands. But the relationship between human beings and the world cannot be such. Human beings do not come from another world, they are a part of this world. The world itself along with its many components constructs human beings.[10]

Human beings cannot impinge their own laws over the laws of the world, because they themselves have been constructed through these very laws. The basic meaning of human beings winning over the world is that they have begun to 'know the world in a more comprehensive manner'.[11] Culture plays a major role in this process, and activists associated with the cultural movement have noted that this cannot be done unless the progressive forces take note of the importance that the folk artists and the folk form hold with regard to their ability to connect with the masses.[12]

Under contemporary capitalism, where progressive individuals have been politically and socially ostracized, it becomes important for the progressive cultural movement to work towards the public recognition of activists which also entails within itself the popularization of these forms of cultural expression. This would then also result in the creation of popular public perception, one of the critical needs of the social justice movement in a country such as India that deals with, especially

---

[10] Chattopadhyaya, D. P. *Sotyer Sondhane Manush*. Kolkata: Anushtup, 1957/2011, p. 57. Trans. Author.

[11] Chattopadhyaya ibid., pp. 57-58. Trans. Author.

[12] Tanvir. H. Interview by J. Malick. In N. Malick & J. Malick (eds), *Habib Tanvir: Reflections and Reminiscences*. New Delhi: SAHMAT, 1995/2010.

regarding issues focused on gender and caste.[13] The public recognition of anti-establishment political figures is an important part of the broader structure of anti-neoliberal politics of the twenty-first century. Recognition brings in different facets of their socio-political and cultural existence to the limelight, a process that extends beyond the immediate context of the form of expression and becomes extremely important under contemporary capitalism where every form of cultural expression has been commoditized.[14] The public recognition of revolutionary poets and activists such as Makhdoom Moinuddin, Dappu Ramesh, and the like is important not only because of their contributions to society as revolutionary artists but also because of the social strata that they come from.

The cultural resistance that stems from individuals coming from the lower strata of society comes after a significant battle against injustices.[15] Even if somebody from the marginalized sections does find space within the artistic circle, it is often overlooked or not critically engaged, and the celebration of such art is often restricted to certain ritualistic or exceptional circumstances.[16] The student's cultural movement has the potential to transform the way in which such individuals are received in the broader society because students occupy the central points of the knowledge dissemination process in society. Because of the students' unique socio-political positioning in society, they have the ability to alter the state of public morality in society which plays a crucial role in the determination of the

---

[13] Jalil, R. *A Rebel and her Cause: The Life and Work of Rashid Jahan*. New Delhi: Women Unlimited, 2014.

[14] Adorno, T. W. 'On the Fetish Character in Music and the Regression of Listening'. In The Culture Industry: Selected Essays on Mass Culture. London: Routledge, 1982/2001.

[15] One can here refer to the autobiography of rapper and student activist Sumeet Samos' autobiography, 'Affairs of Caste' published by Panther's Paw Publications. A review is available here https://scroll.in/article/1028378/anti-caste-rapper-sumeet-samoss-memoir-explores-an-alternate-politics-of-solidarity [Accessed 25.07.2023]

[16] Ilaiah, K. 'Caste, the Artist and the Historian: What Colour is the Nationalist Cow'. In D. Achrar & S. K. Panikkar (eds.), *Articulating Resistance: Art and Activism*. New Delhi: Tulika Books, 2012.

taste of the masses,[17] which becomes extremely important because the South Asian populace has always had an important position reserved for public morality and ethics in its public life.

The common human being's striving for a better life of self-fulfillment made one look towards alternative forms of art.[18] The kind of reality that progressive writers, singers and artists pursue in their work is a direct manifestation of the society that they live in rather than an escapist utopia that makes these works transcend the status of being artifacts and converts them into active political commentary.[19] This remains the core reason behind some of them being completely stripped off from getting any socio-political recognition in India, as two activists explain in great detail:

> We wanted to organize something on the birth anniversary of Makhdoom Moinuddin. The department and the university did not allow that. Twenty years ago, people like Faiz and Jalib were considered untouchable on the campuses, today because the global order has had to recognize them, and their contributions to Pakistan and to the broader South Asian scenario, they are being celebrated. Poets such as Makhdoom or Vilas Ghogre are yet to get due justice in society. (Student Activist, Hyderabad)
>
> Protest songs in Bhojpuri are a rarity. You can find them in contrasting spaces. You can find them either in the rural hinterlands of the country or in the university spaces. The fact that the same kind of songs can be sung in such contrasting spaces makes one realize there is a connection between

---

[17] Ranciere, J. The Intellectual and his People. London: Verso, 2012.

[18] Sengupta, S. 'All Art belongs to the Common Man'. In S. Pradhan (ed.), *Marxist Cultural Movement in India, Volume 2: Chronicles and Documents (1947-1958)*. Kolkata: National Book Agency, 1952/2017.

[19] Chattopadhyay, H. 'Writers and the People'. In S. Pradhan (ed.), *Marxist Cultural Movement in India, Volume 3: Chronicles and Documents (1943-1964)*. Kolkata: National Book Agency, 1953/2017.

the developed and the underdeveloped areas of Indian democracy. The point is to excavate it and relate it to the present context. (Student Cultural Activist, Delhi)

In societies such as India, cultural positioning is deeply ingrained within the civilizational values, which have influenced the decisions that citizens make in their everyday lives. Attributes such as caste, creed, and ethnicity—which have over the centuries become civilizational aspects of the Indian subcontinent—have played a critical role in deciding how the civilization has moved forward since medieval times.[20] This importance of culture is also noted by the far-right, so much so that, a columnist writing on the right-wing website, The Frustrated Indian noted: "The culture of a country decides its politics, the politics of the country decides its defence and economy. Fix culture, and everything else gets fixed automatically."[21] While the un-dialectical approach of the writer needs to be criticized—and quite rightly so—it must be acknowledged that the writer has exposed one of the most important tactics that is being used in contemporary times by the right wing to make inroads into different societies. Be it Donald Trump, Jair Bolsonaro, or Narendra Modi, all of them have invoked certain cultural traits to make themselves heard and accepted within society. Trump made headlines with his speeches on Make America Great Again, while Modi made a spectre out of the Hindu-Muslim fault lines in India during his rise to power. Far-right figures have constantly used cultural and civilizational values to make themselves look relevant in society. In societies such as India, where poverty is at a historic high[22] with added

---

[20] Marcuse, H. Eros and Civilisation. Chicago: Beacon, 1956.

[21] Mishra, A. K. 'The Striking Similarity between Indian Cricket Team of the 90s and Hindus of Today'. *The Frustrated Indian*, 2020, February 28, Para No. 7. Available at: https://www.tfipost.com/2020/02/the-striking-similarity-between-indian-cricket-team-of-the-90s-and-hindus-of-today/

[22] Bhalla, S., Bhasin, K., & Virmani, A. 'Raising the Standard: Time for a Higher Poverty Line in India'. *Brookings*, 2022, April 14. Available at: https://www.brookings.edu/articles/raising-the-standard-time-for-a-higher-poverty-line-in-india/ [Accessed 25.07.2023]

issues such as unemployment, sociocultural backwardness, and illiteracy, the evocation of past glories and history from an antagonistic viewpoint toward leaders and rulers coming from certain communities have a distinct socio-political and cultural effect on the populace. Ramachandra Guha noted that the damages caused by the far-right in India are going to be far more disastrous in form and content than their Western counterparts because the rise of the far-right in the country has been complemented by a completely spine-less media and the relatively stagnant nature of the opposition. Guha writes:

> All demagogues are bad for democracy, but some demagogues are worse than others. If Donald Trump loses next month,[23] America may recover relatively soon from his depredations. Great Britain was shrinking into itself even before Boris Johnson became prime minister; his impact on the history of his country will turn out to be relatively negligible. However, the destruction that Narendra Modi can wreak indeed has already wreaked, on Indian democracy is immense. It will take decades to repair.[24]

In circumstances such as this, escapist art forms do not serve the purpose that it served during times of peace.[25] Sajjad Zaheer, one of the pioneering cultural activists from colonial India, noted that the task of the cultural movement is to provide a break from the mainstream cultural forms, which are often escapist in

---

[23] Article was written in 2020. Donald Trump lost the American Presidential election to Joe Biden in 2020. The same goes to Boris Johnson, who has now been succeeded by Rishi Sunak in Great Britain.

[24] Guha, R. 'A Tale of three Demagogues—and Why Modi is the Most Dangerous to his Country'. Scroll, October 25, 2020. Available at: https://scroll.in/article/976657/ramachandra-guha-a-tale-of-three-demagogues-and-why-modi-is-the-worst [Accessed 25.07.2023]

[25] Ali op cit.

nature[26] and do not challenge the real contradictions of the society that human beings inhabit.[27] Students, and young people in general, occupy an important position in this regard because students remain the most exploited consumers of the kind of culture that capitalism promotes under neoliberalism.[28] Exploiting studenthood is a global affair but has strong local roots. The exploitation of students varies under the context in which it is practiced. The jingoistic cultural nationalism practiced by the BJP has resulted in a gradual saffronization of the campuses—a term that has been used to refer to the constant hate-mongering and Islamophobia that the BJP has promoted across the various campuses of the country.[29] This has created an extraordinary spectrum of issues for students, especially those coming from the marginalized sections of the populace who have found it extremely difficult to voice their concerns within the neoliberal university.[30] In the Third World, where policy reforms have almost always had to follow suit with the Western world, the cultural movement often remains the only space where diverse local political issues can be represented. An activist recounts:

> Most political formations focus on national issues. The cultural movement has that innate ability to tackle those issues that are more intimate to the masses. Take the case of domestic violence. As student activists, it is often the case that when we talk about domestic violence and sexual

---

[26] Zaheer, S. S. (1936/2017). A Note on the Progressive Writers' Association. In S. Pradhan (ed.), *Marxist Cultural Movement in India, Volume 1: Chronicles and Documents (1936-1947)*. Kolkata: National Book Agency.

[27] Sengupta ibid.

[28] Giroux, H. Neoliberalism's War on Higher Education. Chicago: Haymarket, 2014.

[29] Puniyani, R. 'Saffronization of Education: A Blueprint to Build Hindu Rashtra'. In N. Narayanan, & D. Dhar (eds), *Education or Exclusion: The Plight of Indian Students*. New Delhi: Leftword, 2022.

[30] Genriel, D. 'Rhodes must Fall: Oxford and Movements for Change'. In G. K. Bhambra, D. Gabrial, & K. Nisancioglu (eds.), *Decolonising the University*. London: Pluto Press, 2018; Holmwood, J. 'Race and the Neoliberal University: Lessons from the Public University'. In G. K. Bhambra, D. Gabrial, & K. Nisancioglu (eds.), *Decolonising the University*. London: Pluto Press, 2018.

harassment on the campus, the question that comes is how is that relevant to the campus? When we perform a play or a song, these questions seem relevant, because the students can relate to them. (Cultural Student Activist, Bangalore)

True to the words of the activist, the progressive cultural movement has always been an important part of the way in which the debates surrounding global politics have been framed in the context of the Third World, especially in the articulation and exertion of ways in which such issues can be related to the local context. In this context, Rakshanda Jalil writes:

> The PWM and its proponents were a powerful and inescapable force commandeering a space for themselves on the political, social, and literary canvas of India for nearly three decades. In the years before Independence, they influenced the debates on imperialism and decolonization, and in the years after, they were at the centre of the discourses on the nature of the newly independent, post-colonized state and society.[31]

There are two reasons that can be said to lay behind this dramatic rise of the cultural movement in India. The first point is regarding the question of literacy and the second relates to the idea of material progress and its relationship to ideology. In India, the literacy rate in 1947 was around 12%, and by 1981 it had only increased to around 43.5%.[32] Even in 2022, the literacy

---

[31] Jalil, R. *Liking Progress, Loving Change: A Literary History of the Progressive Writers' Movement in Urdu*. New Delhi: Oxford University Press, 2020, p. 2.

[32] See https://www.oxfamindia.org/featuredstories/10-facts-illiteracy-india-you-must-know#:~:text=After%20the%20end%20of%20the,importance%20of%20education%20for%20all [Accessed 25.07.2023]; Sarker, K. 'Economic Growth and Social Inequality: Does the Trickle-Down Effect Really Take Place'. *New Proposals: Journal of Marxism and Interdisciplinary Inquiry*, 3(1), 2009, 42-60.

rate has been just 77.7%.[33] The lower literacy rates mean that people at large often do not possess the language that is required to articulate their opinions and voices. People from the lower classes, lower castes and marginalized races—and especially the women among them—are left at the mercy of the leaders of their communities to voice their concerns. And, it can be said without much reasonable doubt that in most cases, the interests of the leaders rarely match with those of the led. There are intricate circuits of capital, power and domination involved that create a gulf between the leaders and the led, creating a situation where the masses merely exist as cannon fodder for the leaders to fill up the numbers. Cultural politics can provide a unique framework within which potentially sensitive issues can be discussed and brought in front of the public—and most importantly, in a language that the public understands and can relate to without much effort. It is the unique nature of cultural politics that can be used by progressive political formations—which include political parties, student groups, women's organizations, and others—to build alliances and construct bridges across different spectrums of radical dissenting voices and progressive identity politics. For example, in regions such as India's North-East, which have historically been at the receiving end of structural violence from mainstream India, cultural politics occupies an important position. Plagued by the effects of uneven development, the northeastern region of India has always been at the receiving end of different kinds of exclusionary measures[34]—both economic and cultural that have been highly problematic, especially for the students.[35] A cultural activist from one North-Eastern state argued:

---

[33] See https://timesofindia.indiatimes.com/education/news/international-literacy-day-2022-theme-significance-history/articleshow/94065106.cms# [Accessed 25.07.2023]

[34] Prasad, P. H. 'Roots of Uneven Regional Growth in India'. *Economic and Political Weekly*, *23*(33), 1988, 1968-92.

[35] Das, S. 'How do they continue to fail the people from the North-eastern States'. In N. Narayanan & D. Dhar (eds.), *Education of Exclusion: The Plight of Indian Students*. New Delhi: Leftword, 2022.

> Culture gives a voice to me. It does not objectivize me as a human being but rather allows me to be in the driver's seat. It stops the tendency of dehumanization of the people of North-East, something that is so common in mainstream culture and even the politics that originate from that. When we sing in our language about our land about our problems, we become autonomous subjects. (Cultural Student Activist, Manipur-Delhi)

The evocation of cultural resistance in such regions has often been a strong part of the broader movement for social justice. University students' organizing of events such as 'Nights of Resistance' has a wider socio-political meaning that traverses beyond the immediate socio-political contexts. In doing so, the student activists not only present a model to society but also counter the contradictions that often exist within their own organizations. One activist states:

> Performing plays at night is often more revolutionary in nature than doing a protest. Cultural activism still attracts very few women. There are very few woman student activists, even today. Among them, if somebody comes within the cultural troupe, it is our responsibility to make them aware of their agency, and that includes their right over the night. (Cultural Student Activist, Delhi)

The emphasis on the participation of women and Dalits becomes critical because women tend to face more attacks on themselves and their loved ones if they go against the norms set by society.[36] While the mainstream political discourse often treats these individuals as mere objects,[37] the cultural resistance provides the actors involved with a sense of being a subject. Modes of cultural resistance provide individuals with the necessary ideological

---

[36] Jalil ibid.

[37] Weeks, K. *Constructing Feminist Subjects*. London: Verso, 2018; Teltumbde, A. *The Republic of Caste*. New Delhi: Navayana, 2018.

arsenal through which they act in opposition to the state of technological rationality that is constructed by the objectification of the labor power of the working people by a process of complete and inhuman 'reification of human labor power'.[38] Resisting through cultural expressions enables them to resist their own objectification that is produced by the universalization of the commodity form under capitalism that shapes the social structure and the relations therein with most social relations reduced to their quantitative relations that are governed by objective laws independently of the will and desire of the agents involved in the process.[39] Unfortunately, a significant section of the cultural groups operating within the various campuses also have been affected by the same.

Historian, K. N. Panikkar noted that one of the major issues with cultural troupes is the amount of control that mainstream political formations exert over them.[40] Most cultural organizations and troupes have functioned as front or mass organizations of larger vanguardist political formations. Vanguardism, as a concept, has always been an important one in the context of South Asia. The idea that a socially developed and well-connected community would need to be the leaders of a social transformation has been deeply entrenched within the Indian belief system—which often stems from the beliefs surrounding caste, gender, race, and ethnicity. Vanguardism is understood as 'the selection of a group of single-minded revolutionaries prepared to make any sacrifice, from the more or less chaotic mass of the class as a whole'.[41] How vanguardism was implemented in India was constructed out of the militarized Leninism that was implemented in states such as China and Vietnam (Löfgren, 2016), one that becomes apparent in the work of Mazumdar (1965/2020), in the process of ascertaining the importance of the local context in organizational activities

---

[38] Marcuse, H. *One-Dimensional Man*. London: Routledge, 1964/2002, p. 36, 40

[39] Lukacs, G. History and Class Consciousness. Massachusetts MA: MIT Press, 1923/1977.

[40] Panikkar, K. N. 'Progressive Cultural Movement in India: A Critical Appraisal'. In *The Progressive Cultural Movement: A Critical History*. New Delhi: SAHMAT, 2017.

[41] Lukacs op cit., p. 25.

constructed an ideological position dominated by a complete demonization of individual subjectivity, and in the analysis of regional statist bureaucracies in India.[42]

Hegemonic control includes the structuring of the everyday lives of common people and the organizations that they form (Ives, 2014). However, while the idea of the importance of everyday life and hegemonic control is attributed to thinkers such as Henri Lefebvre in France (1991) and Antonio Gramsci in Italy (1977), Bhagat Singh and his comrades at the HSRA had enshrined these issues in a political sense in its constitution during the 1910s and early 1920s itself. The contemporary cultural movement in India manifests such important steps taken by the early progenitors of the social justice movement in the country. Progressive poetry and the songs of resistance, which often emanate from them, have been an integral part of the students' movement in India. Political groups on different campuses regularly use culture to make themselves heard on the campuses. While organizations such as PTG and Dastak have been functioning with complete freedom on campuses across the country, at the end of the day, they remain under the ideological guidance of the larger political formations within their respective campuses. Mainstream political formations retain a considerable hold over these formations, which translates to them often being controlled by mainstream political formations despite not being formally affiliated with them.

Students have been an important section of the non-capitalist class in India and have been, historically speaking, at the forefront of struggles focused on ensuring social justice in India.[43] Be it within the decades that followed the independence of the country from colonial rule during the 1960s and 1970s when the entire nation was coming to terms with heightened radicalism among the students and civil society or after 1991 when the country was put at the mercy of neoliberalism, students have been an important factor among the broad array of actors

---

[42] Nossiter, T. J. *Marxist State Governments in India*. London: Printer Publishers, 1988.

[43] Rajimwale, A. History of Student Movements in India: Origins and Development. New Delhi: Manjul, 2001.

who had been instrumental in bringing out the demerits and the potentially disastrous aftereffects associated with those moves. The broad assertion of cultural politics within the campuses takes root from the idea that university spaces are some of the most vibrant spaces in any society. This is, in spite, of the fact that such spaces are highly unreal in nature in the sense that they rarely emulate the values that have become mainstream in society outside the walls of the campuses. It is natural that important and contemporary issues will find a space for getting discussed and debated in these spaces, even though the impact of these debates might be limited—and truth be told, without much of a political domino effect as well.

The art and politics of cultural resistance has been an important part of the students' movement in India. The students' movement in India, has historically, encompassed within itself diverse tendencies within the broader social justice movement. It has represented a diverse admixture of tendencies that have often been completely marginalized in the mainstream political discourse. In the realm of general politics, the progressive cultural movement has influenced almost all sections of society, even though the magnitude of those effects might have been different.[44] This has even been felt within the realm of the broader progressive cultural politics, especially when IPTA—for the first time—received fraternal greetings from other fraternal revolutionary organizations of the time, such as the All-India Trade Union Congress (AITUC), the All India Students' Federation (AISF) and the Progressive Writers' Association (PWA) in its sixth conference. In the sixth All India Conference of the IPTA:

> The IPTA ... declared itself to be on the side of the democratic, anti-imperialist camp—to be a comrade-in-arms in the struggle for democracy and socialism waged by peasants, workers and intellectuals. IPTA has pledged to develop the movement on these principles: 1. The People's Theatre movement should be consciously and

---

[44] Jalil, R. *Liking Progress, Loving Change: A Literary History of the Progressive Writers' Movement in Urdu*. New Delhi: Oxford University Press, 2020.

> relentlessly built up through the struggles of the different sections of the people and through day-to-day movements for democracy[;] 2. It shall build up a resistance movement against reactionary views and attacks on cultural movements. It shall combat the economic crisis in the lives of the exploited, professional artists and writers and the consequent prostitution of their talents to reactionary forces. Through the movement, it shall unite the artists under the banner of the democratic front.[45]

These statements are important ones in the context of the cultural movement in India because they signify the ways in which the cultural movement had initially been conceptualized in free India, which was in synchronization with the broader politics of social justice as was envisaged by the members of the IPTA—most of whom were also involved quite intimately with the social justice movements of the country. Protest theatre and songs, as one activist put it, have often occupied an important position in the way in which the movements have articulated their demands and ideological contours in society. They have been instrumental, as some go on to claim, in fulfilling some of the responsibilities that the state ought to have performed such as the unfinished business of women's participation in the society.

> The question is why we do plays in front of the ladies' hostel. I think more than opportunism or other things, this is our responsibility. Historically, the society has always oppressed women. They have restricted their mobility, their access, and their life. When we finish our round of plays or performances in front of the ladies' hostel at say 12 or 1 AM at night, we are not only critiquing the society but also

---

[45] Indian Peoples' Theatre Association. (1951). The Sixth All India Conference of the Indian Peoples' Theatre Association. In S. Pradhan (ed.), *Marxist Cultural Movement in India, Volume 2: Chronicles and Documents (1947-1958)*. Kolkata: National Book Agency, 1951/2017, p. 50.

Cultural activities enable the diversification of the movement as a whole. In campuses such as JNU or UOH, the diversification of the movement becomes a crucial factor because of how the demography of the campus has been constructed over the years in terms of the regions, ethnicities and social demographics, in addition to social attributes such as class, caste, gender and race. Cultural activities in such kinds of social settings, help the progressive forces in gaining influence among sections coming from regions devoid of any strong left-wing political and social presence. The activist recounts:

> There was a serious lack of activists coming in from regions such as Assam, Manipur, Odisha, etc. in the organization. But then we decided that in our cultural performances, we would integrate their culture while still retaining a healthy distance from completely appropriating them. We learned some of the songs, did not understand most of them, but still attempted to sing them. This helped us immensely in building a connection with them. We now have more than twenty percent of our membership from those regions. (Student Activist, Delhi)

Modes of cultural protest play an important role in how the larger debates about the relevance of the same are structured within mainstream thought. Culture is something that is far more encompassing and inclusive in nature than economics. However, culture alone will not serve the purpose. Marginalized sections of the population require both economic prowess and cultural assertion to make themselves heard and then move towards higher levels of analytical abstraction to counter aspects such as sexual violence, casteism, racism, and the like, amidst the chaos neoliberal capitalism produces.[46]

---

[46] Diawara, M. 'Black Studies, Cultural Studies: Performative Acts'. In J. Storey (ed), *What is Cultural Studies: A Reader*. London: Arnold, 1997.

6

Articulating Everyday Contradictions

Maiñ ke ek mehnat-kash, maiñ ke teeragi dushman
Subh-e nau ibaarat hai, mere muskuraane se
Surkh inquilaab aaya, daur-e aaftaab aaya
Muntazir thi ye aankheñ jis ki ek zamaane se
Ab zameen gaayegi, hal ke saaz par naghme
Vaadiyoñ meiñ naachenge har taraf taraane se
Manchale bunenge ab rang-o boo ke pairaahan
Ab sañvar ke niklega, husn kaarkhaane se!

Majrooh

[I am a worker, I am the enemy of darkness, My smile is what brings about the new morning, The red revolution arrives, that day of brightness dawns, Which these eyes have been awaiting for so long. Now the earth will sing songs to the beat of the plough. Anthems will dance in the valleys. The carefree will weave garments of colour and fragrance And beauty shall emerge, adorned, from within the factory walls, Calling a spade a spade: the poetry of bluntness] 1

Life, expression, and emotions are the basic fulcrums around which one builds an aesthetic sense of one's life.[2] Exploitation

---

[1] Mir & Mir op cit., p. p. 36.

[2] Ranciere 2012 op cit.

thus only becomes exploitation in reality because of it being rooted within everyday social interactions,[3] where it can interfere with how one life, expresses, and feels—which are extremely subjective factors. This warrants an understanding of exploitation that not only critiques the attempts to quantify the qualitative aspects of human life and establish a regime of standardization under capitalism[4] but also provides the pathways towards a more egalitarian mode of developing a transformative egalitarian sociopolitical theory because human beings do not struggle against the State or Capitalism in their everyday lives. Rather their struggles in their everyday lives remain against the manifestations of these concepts in their everyday lives that take place mostly in the form of regular everyday issues.[5] In the daily life of Indians, issues such as communalism and caste hatred do not feature as concepts or grand events but rather they do so as mundane everyday processes. Speaking on the nature of the mundane everyday life and its critical importance for analyzing social reality, Henri Lefebvre writes:

> Everyday life ... defined by "what is left over" after all distinct superior, specialised, structured activities have been singled out for analysis, must be defined as a totality. Considered in their specialisation and their technicality, superior activities leave a "technical vacuum" between one another which is filled by everyday life. Everyday life is profoundly related to all activities, and encompasses them with all their differences and their conflicts; it is their meeting place, their bond, their common ground.[6]

---

[3] Rathod, B. *Dalit Academic Journeys: Stories of Caste, Exclusion and Assertion in Indian Higher Education*. Abingdon: Routledge, 2023.

[4] Marcuse, H. 'Some Social Implications of Modern Technology'. In D. Kellner (ed), *Collected Papers of Herbert Marcuse: Volume 1*. London: Routledge, 1941/1998; Marcuse, H. 'From Ontology to Technology'. In D. Kellner & C. Pierce (eds.), *Collected Papers of Herbert Marcuse: Volume 5*. London: Routledge, 1960/2011.

[5] Soper, K. *Post-Growth Living*. London: Verso, 2020.

[6] Lefebvre, H. *Critique of Everyday Life: Volume 1*. London: Verso, 1991, p. 97.

It is this mundane everyday life that cultural activism is mostly associated with. Analyzing culture needs to consider its all-encompassing nature and its role in different facets of human life, especially in contexts such as South Asia, where economics and culture are more intimately woven with each other than most other countries of the West. The onslaught of capitalist industrialization was one of the basic underlying causes behind the rendering mainstream of real subsumption in the 19th century characterized by a rise of money capital and wage labor that changed the base associated with a pre-capitalist or feudal society. The development of capitalism in such cases occurs through a transformation of the relations and means of production in the society that causes a disruption within the traditional superstructure(s) of any pre-capitalist society by altering the material, social and ideal forms often assumed by the socio-economic content.[7] In such societies, it is often the adherence to social customs by most of the workers and poor populace that becomes the basis of advanced industrial production.[8] The adherence to social customs in any society is a cultural affair, one which becomes highly contradictory in societies such as India, which are plagued by a combination of both pre-capitalist customs that dictate its social fabric and the capitalist economic structure that it so desperately desires to be a part of.[9] The transformation of the character of an egalitarian political formation depends upon how it conceives of the dialectics between the pre-capitalist social formations and the capitalist ones,[10] within which culture plays a critical role in the

---

[7] De Smet, B. *Gramsci on Tahrir: Revolution and Counter-Revolution in Egypt*. London: Pluto Press, 2016.

[8] Dobb, M. 'A Note on Theories of Development and Underdevelopment'. In A. R. Desai (ed), *Essays on Modernization of Underdeveloped Societies: Volume 1*. New York: Humanities Press, 1972.

[9] Myrdal, G. *Asian Drama: An Inquiry into the Poverty of Nations*. London: Allen Lane, 1968.

[10] Marx, K. *The Ethnological Notebooks of Karl Marx*. Amsterdam: Van Gorcum and Company, 1974; Green, M. 'Gramsci cannot Speak: Presentations and Interpretations of Gramsci's Concept of the Subaltern'. Rethinking Marxism, 14(3), 2002, 1-24.

context of South Asia. Culture shapes how people are sought to be administered by those in positions of power and is often as important as aspects of the economy[11] in the everyday life of the nation. Speaking about the relationship between culture and administration, Adorno noted:

> Whoever speaks of culture speaks of administration as well, whether this is his intention or not. The combination of so many things lacking a common denominator—such as philosophy and religion, science and art, forms of conduct and mores—and finally the inclusion of the objective spirit of an age in the single word "culture" betrays from the outset the administrative view, the task of which, looking down from on high, is to assemble, distribute, evaluate and organize.[12]

Adorno here highlights the emancipatory role that culture can play provided it is managed in a way that it can do so. Different progressive groups have come to understand the cultural struggle in various ways. The most pervasive definition of cultural struggle is one that considers the fact that cultural resistance is both an entity and a process in itself, where modes of expression are used both as a medium as well as an artifact in expressing resistance and dissent against the status quo.[13] Within the contours of the student struggles in India, this becomes evident by the fact that cultural modes of expressing dissent have not only been a process through which students have been able to bring forth a new way of interpreting traditional cultural forms, but also establish newer forms of resistance that is simultaneously progressively patriotic and internationalist, and anti-capitalist. Being all of these necessarily entails within itself a counter-argument to the:

---

[11] Patnaik, P. 'Politics, Culture and Socialism'. In *The Progressive Cultural Movement: A Critical History*. New Delhi: SAHMAT, 2017.

[12] Adorno, T. W. 'Culture and Administration'. In *The Culture Industry: Selected Essays on Mass Culture*. London: Routledge, 1978/2001, p. 107.

[13] Duncombe, S. '(From) Cultural Resistance to Community Development'. Community Development Journal, 42(4), 2007, 490-500.

[r]igid institutionalization [of culture that] transforms modern mass culture into a medium of undreamed-of psychological control. The repetitiveness, the selfsameness, and the ubiquity of modern mass culture tend of make for automatized reactions and to weaken the forces of individual resistance ... The increasing strength of modern mass culture is further enhanced by changes in the sociological structure of the audience. The old cultural elite no longer exists; the modern intelligentsia only partially corresponds to it. At the same time, huge strata of the population formerly unacquainted with art have become cultural "consumers".[14]

Turning back to the folk and progressive roots of the cultural movement has enabled the movement to bring back the sense of community that contributes to the radical aesthetics associated with these forms of cultural expression.[15] Singer-activists such as Poojan Sahil, who shot to fame during the anti-CAA protests, have proved that it is possible to break the capitalist hegemony over art forms by imagining newer forms of internationalist renditions of classical protest songs—such as his 'Wapas Jao!', an Indianized version of 'Bella Ciao'[16] that became almost an anthem of the 2020-2021 Farmers' protests in India.[17] Or, one can take the example of Aamir Aziz's poem 'Sab Yaad Rakha Jayega' [Everything will be Remembered] was so popular and powerful that even George Roger Waters of Pink Floyd recited this at one of his public events expressing solidarity with the protests against the CAA-NRC in India.[18] Contemporary protest

---

[14] Adorno, T. W. 'Television and the Patterns of Mass Culture'. In B. Rosenberg & D. M. White (eds.), *Mass Culture: The Popular Arts in America*. New York: Free Press, 1957, p. 476.

[15] Patnaik op cit.

[16] The Video can be accessed here https://www.youtube.com/watch?v=NJJoVMIQeCw [Accessed 25.07.2023]

[17] See https://www.thequint.com/my-report/india-pakistan-iaf-strikes-war-loc-attacks [Accessed 25.07.2023]

[18] See https://www.youtube.com/watch?v=Dco4fNM33Sk [Accessed 25.07.2023]

music in India has thus evolved into becoming staunchly internationalist in nature. This can also be seen in how Indian students have used poets such as Faiz and Jalib during the 2016-2017 JNU students' movement against sedition as well during the recent anti-CAA protests, where the students played a critical role, and protest music achieved new heights. It was important to note that while the singers were Indian, the songs that they mostly sang were almost all penned by Pakistani poets —or what came to be Pakistan after 1947. The kind of internationalism that the student movement has exhibited in India is an exemplary one—it has simultaneously resisted the jingoistic nationalism of the BJP as well as provided a new lease of life to internationalism within the Indian students' movement.

> During the recent wave of student movements in the country, the country seemed back like how it used to be during the 1970s, with people singing about Vietnam and about China and about Russia that we have heard about. The kind of songs and poems that were being recited made us remember the 70s. The students were reciting Faiz and Jalib and Woody Guthrie and Paul Robeson and showing solidarity with the Black Lives Matter movement. All of this shows that we are indeed a part of the larger international movement against social injustice. (Cultural Student Activist, Bangalore)

The same goes for ideas about liberation. Students have been able to invoke the spirit of liberation much more eloquently than other sections of the populace whenever they have attempted to do so through the utilization of culture. Take the now iconic play, 'O' Womaniya' by the Progressive Theatre Group (PTG) at the University of Hyderabad, as an example. The play has been a major blockbuster in the university space which otherwise does not talk kindly to those involved in the realm of direct left-wing and progressive politics on the campus.[19] This play was first staged on the University of Hyderabad campus and has since

---

[19] Singh et al. op cit.

been performed innumerable times, including some invited performances even outside the campus. The play and its associated success denoted that when articulated in a manner that is accessible to all and portrayed in a fashion that is easily understandable, most issues such as women's security and sexual harassment can in fact strike a chord with a highly apolitical audience. One performer associated with the play noted:

> 'O' Womaniya was so popular that even people from outside the campus invite us to do shows of the play. In fact, even after so many years, we still get requests to perform the same play over and over again sometimes even from some of the academic departments. This is exemplary. This shows that once you have a good play or a good song, you will be noticed and you will be appreciated. (Cultural Activist, Hyderabad)

These plays, along with regular performances by the PTG have become commonplace in the campus life of the university. Over the past few years, the PTG has performed plays on diverse topics, including the centenary celebration of the 1917 Russian Revolution. The play on the 1917 Russian Revolution involved more than 25 actors, the highest ever in the decade-long history of the cultural troupe. In fact, the success that the PTG has enjoyed in the UOH has become an exemplary one in universities and campuses nationally because the PTG's political affiliations did not come in the way of it gaining social acceptance in the campus. As one of the founding members puts it:

> PTG is an example. It is unthinkable that a cultural group affiliated directly with a political organization has survived so long on a campus where the RSS and the BJP have launched constant attacks. The fact that we have been successful speaks volumes about the kind of work that we and the broader organization have done. PTG has been a force on the campus, which echoes the voices of countless students who are either too afraid or too reluctant to join the mainstream students'

movement. It helps us to make inroads into sections where we do not have much social belonging, as well as enables us to bring newer issues to the forefront which is at times very difficult to articulate in political terms.

One of the many reasons for the success of politico-cultural organizations such as the PTG is that they have worked as a bridge between the 'apolitical' students and the political discourses on the campus. In fact, that has been the dominant discourse in most campuses across the country. The success of groups such as the PTG in gaining momentum among the students is related to how it echoes the voices and sentiments of the students who otherwise do not find themselves engaged directly with political activities. An activist recounted to the author:

For me, the cultural movement is extremely important as far as the movement of Dalits, minorities and women are concerned. While the conventional left has often not been able to voice their opinions and conditions of life in their day-to-day politics, the cultural movement has done that quite effectively. It has also made many realize that we too exist and that you cannot have a movement that neglects the reality of half of the population. (Student Activist, Delhi)

These narratives from different activists prove that cultural resistance plays an important role in how individuals frame their own existence within these spaces. How students express themselves in campus spaces is a culmination of both the ideological effect that such a space has on them and their material reality—one which is often at complete odds with the campus space. This becomes one of the basic fulcrums around which they begin to constitute their subjective selfhood in such spaces. In other words, there is a crucial relationship between culture and selfhood. As Marcuse had noted:

> Culture is a realm of mind. A social or political institutions, a work of art, a religion, and a philosophical system exist and operate as part and parcel of man's own being, products of a rational subject that continues to live in them. As products

they constitute an objective realm; at the same time, they are subjective, created by human beings. They represent the possible unity of subject and object. The development of culture shows distinct stages that denote different levels of relation between man and his world, that is, different ways of apprehending and mastering the world and of adapting it to human needs and potentialities.[20]

Modes of cultural resistance become popular because they intersect with the ontological basis of human life, more so under the aegis of total institutions such as a university or a factory that work based on restricting their freedom and putting them within an administered way of life.[21] However, it must be mentioned here that even though what PTG does is political art, it does not manifest itself as an overtly political organization, but rather it continues to be seen as just a part of the larger political formations in place. This tendency is not an alien concept in contemporary social theory and analysis which tends to focus more on the role that larger structures have in the process of ensuring social justice often completely relegating the critical role that smaller formations and activities play in the path towards liberation.[22] A more nuanced analysis requires an understanding of the internal and external contradictions existing in the society that go beyond mere economistic understanding and analysis of the society and analyze the questions centered upon cultural, political, and social issues analyzing their intersections.[23] The overemphasis on meta-theory often disregards the role that individuals and individualism play in constructing political

---

[20] Marcuse, H. *Reason and Revolution: Hegel and the Rise of Social Theory*. London: Routledge and Kegan Paul Limited, 1955, p. 56.

[21] Goffman, E. *Asylums: essays on the social situation of mental patients and other inmates*. New York: Anchor Books, 1961.

[22] Morton. A. D. Unravelling Gramsci: Hegemony and Passive Revolution in the Global Political Economy. London: Pluto Press, 2007; Cox, L. 'The Southern Question and the Irish Question: A Social Movement Perspective'. In Ó. G. Agustin, & M. B. Jørgensen (eds.), *Solidarity without Borders*. London: Pluto Press, 2016.

[23] Boothman, D. 'Political and Social Alliances: Gramsci and Today'. In Ó. G. Agustin, & M. B. Jørgensen (eds.), *Solidarity without Borders*. London: Pluto Press, 2016.

subjects and communities.[24] The emancipation of the individual subjectivity means the establishment of the human being as an individual in the truest sense of the term whose individual existence might differ from the social existence that the same person possesses, and not simply as a citizen[25]—a trend that has grown considerably under the Hindutva regime.

---

[24] Marcuse, H. 'The Individual in the Great Society'. In D. Kellner (ed), *Collected Papers of Herbert Marcuse: Volume 2*. London: Routledge, 1966/2001; Warren, M. E. 'Marx and Methodological Individualism'. In T. Carver & P. Thomas (eds.), *Rational Choice Marxism*. London: Palgrave Macmillan, 1995.

[25] Marcuse, H. *The Aesthetic Dimension: Toward a Critique of Marxist Aesthetics*. Boston: Beacon Press, 1977; Vanaik 2018 op cit.

7
Cultural Resistance and Revolutionary Subjectivity

Tum Raat Likho Hum Chand Likhenge,
Tum Jail Mein Dalo Hum Deewar Phand Likhenge,
Tum FIR Likho Hum Hain Taiyar Likhenge,
Tum Humein Qatl Kar Do Hum Banke Bhoot Likhenge,
Tumhare Qatl Ke Sare Saboot Likhenge,

Aur Tum Adalaton Se Baith Kar Chutkule Likho,
Hum Sadkon Deewaron Pe Insaf Likhenge,
Behre Bhi Sun Le Itni Zor Se Bolenge,
Andhe Bhi Padh Lein Itna Saf Likhenge,
Tum Kala Kamal Likho, Hum Lal Gulab Likhenge,
Tum Zameen Pe Zulm Likh Do,
Asman Pe Inquilab Likha Jayega! ...
— Aamir Aziz

[You could write the night, but we will write the moon. If you put us in jail, we would jump over the walls and still write. You could write FIRs;[1] we will write that we are ready. You could murder us; we will continue to write even after we become ghosts. We will write all the evidence of your crimes. You may enjoy jokes sitting in the courts, but we will ink the walls and roads about the justice we need. We will speak loud enough so even hearing-impaired ones can hear us. You write the Black Lotus, we will write the Red Rose, you can write the land with injustices, The Revolution will be written in the skies.][2]

---

[1] First Information Report: the first procedural report about a crime in India.
[2] Full song available from https://lyricspapa.in/sab-yaad-rakha-jayega-lyrics-english-translation-aamir-aziz/ [Accessed on 28.08.2023]. Translation partly done by the author.

For a country such as India, where heretical beliefs often dictate social and political conditions, adherence to mainstream traditions sometimes acts as a major hurdle towards effecting social transformation. A transformed society would need institutions and policies that are developed by individuals who are characterized by a new set of needs, goals, and desires.[3] These subjective factors play a critical role in constructing an idea of social transformation. The analysis of culture is an important one for progressive individuals because it has the potential to reveal the very core of the entire social organization within which it took shape.[4] Movements and politics based on a cultural mode of resistance make it possible for social movements to take note of the dogmatic assumptions that plague the contemporary theory and praxis in India. It allows them to take cognizance of the fact that the global mode of oppression is related intimately to the local and contextual mode of production and that all societies can 'choose a different path'[5] and a different route towards liberation.

Cultural Resistance has been an important aspect of the anti-capitalist movement since the beginning of the 1960s, when young activists had begun to unearth new meanings of the old terms creating newer kinds of theoretical paradigms based on their experiences.[6] Capitalism came to understand that mere economic suppression would not be able to diffuse the wave of social movements which were mostly being led by young people.

---

[3] Marcuse, H. 'Liberation from the Affluent Society'. In D. Kellner (ed.), *Collected Papers of Herbert Marcuse: Volume 3*. London: Routledge, 1967/2005.

[4] Williams, R. The Long Revolution. London: Verso, 1961/2019.

[5] Dunayevskaya, R. 'Marx and Engels' Studies Contrasted: Relationship of Philosophy and Revolution to Women's Liberation'. In *The Raya Dunayevskaya Collection—Marxist-Humanism: A Half Century of its World Development*. Detroit: Wayne State University Archives of Labor and Urban Affairs, 1979; Dunayevskaya, R. 'Marxist-Humanism: The Summation That is a New Beginning, Subjectively and Objectively'. In P. Hudis, & K. B. Anderson (eds.), *The Power of Negativity: Selected Writings on the Dialectic in Hegel and Marx by Raya Dunayevskaya*. New York: Lexington Books, 1983/2002, p. 259.

[6] Elbaum, M. *Revolution in the Air: Sixties Radicals turn to Lenin, Mao and Che*. London: Verso, 2018.

A few decades later—during the turbulent 60s—the February 19, 1968, issue of the popular magazine Newsweek reported, 'Almost all urban specialists agree: all signs point to a grim summer of riots in the nation's cities ... They note: (1) cuts and restrictions in federal programs for the jobless; (2) a hardening of white-black antipathies; (3) a growing police emphasis on repression and weaponry'. After merely three years, the pro-capital business magazine, Business Week stated on May 16, 1970, 'The invasion of Cambodia and the senseless shooting of four students at Kent State University in Ohio have consolidated the academic community against the war, against business and against the government. This is a dangerous situation. It threatens the whole economic and social structure of the nation'.[7] There is an intimate relationship that exists between student politics and mainstream politics that becomes explicit through the fears expressed in these statements.

Student movements have long been the foundation stones for mainstream political and social activism. These movements have provided the mainstream political formations with innumerable activists and intellectuals, many of whom have gone on to represent the parties in the Indian parliament. The critical importance of student politics in a democracy such as India is not so much in the processes through which it contributes to increasing the number of political figures and intellectuals but rather lies in the contributions that it makes to the overall process of democratization and decentralization in the country. Student movements and activists employ various methods to make their voices heard and recognized within the wider political milieu in the country. Cultural modes of expression and protest play a critical role in the ways in which the student movement of the country addresses issues such as gender violence, caste exploitation, etc. It is often the case that individuals find it easier to express themselves within student politics than in the mainstream political discourse because while the latter is laden with political rationalization, the former is often free from such issues.

---

[7] Ibid.

Sociologist David Brain quite correctly noted that culture occupies a diverse, and often conflicting space, in contemporary political and social processes, one that is dictated by a tussle between interpretation and explanation.[8] Likewise, any form of activism, especially those that are cultural in form and content, is a multi-layered process where different facets of an individual's personality are exposed to and react to different layers and kinds of exploitation and objectification under contemporary capitalism. Culture plays an important role in the process because culture too is a multi-layered entity which 'one [can peel] off layer after layer, each such layer being complete and irreducible in itself, revealing another, quite a different sort of layer underneath'.[9] It not only plays an important role in the integration of ideas on a global scale but also comes to play a significant role in the development of the necessary tools of articulation. This becomes particularly critical in the context of India because of the constantly increasing marginalization that a great many people in the country have been facing because of the neoliberal policies implemented and sustained with greater veracity by succeeding governments since 1991. Neoliberal policies result in higher rates of unemployment which then go on to affect the social structure in place, especially in societies such as India,[10] where processes of urbanization and modernization have produced extremely deplorable circumstances where the marginalized populace has had to endure extraordinary hardships leading to many of them having to live in conditions

---

[8] Brain, D. 'Cultural Production as 'Society in the Making': Architecture as an Exemplar of the Social Construction of Cultural Artifacts'. In D. Crane (ed), *The Sociology of Culture: Emerging Theoretical Perspectives*. London: Blackwell, 1994.
[9] Geertz, C. *The Interpretation of Cultures: Selected Essays*. New York: Basic Books, 1973, p. 37.
[10] Sirohi, R. From Developmentalism to Neoliberalism: A Comparative Analysis of Brazil and India. London: Palgrave Macmillan, 2019; Jha, M. K., & Pankaj, A. K. 'Neoliberal Governmentality and Social Policymaking in India: Implications for In/Formal Workers and Community Work'. *The International Journal of Community and Social Development*, *3*(3), 2021, 198-214.

deemed unsuitable for dignified human life.[11] Such deplorable conditions of sustenance go on to affect not only their economic conditions but also their socio-cultural positions and their aspirations. The effect that the degrading conditions of life have on individuals is pertinent to the sustenance of contemporary capitalism that is characterized by a '[dominance] of the capital-development synergy [which] has an "absolute" and uniform surface, where shopping malls, special economic zones (SEZs), and sky-hugging towers flourish, and which increasingly seem to be rejecting the subaltern "other" that is poor, underfed, disgruntled, and displaced, and hence, not part of this "developed" landscape'.[12] Not being part of the developed landscape—both materially that often includes the rural populace and ideologically that includes women, Dalits, minorities and the like—often puts these individuals into disadvantaged spaces as far as their ability to voice their concerns is concerned.

Analyzing a cultural movement or any form of cultural resistance requires one to take cognizance of the fact that in the domain of culture, it is quite difficult to find absolutes and 'unbroken continuities'—as Stuart Hall put it.[13] Radical and progressive modes of expression break off from the mainstream mode of articulation and propose an entirely new way of looking at society. It is true that individuals are often troubled by the structural restrictions in place that often make them turn towards a sort of stagnancy in their social lives.[14] But, at the same time, it is also true that the very progress of human society is based on human beings transcending these restrictions.[15] This point becomes clearer if one takes the example of women in the students' cultural movement. Under a system dominated by

---

[11] Farooqui, A. *Opium City: The Making of Early Victorian Bombay*. Gurgaon: Three Essays Collective, 2006.

[12] Parasuraman, S. *Economic Liberalization, Informalization of Labour and Social Protection in India*. New Delhi: Aakar, 2010, pp. 1-2.

[13] Hall, S. 'Cultural Studies: Two Paradigms'. In J. Storey (ed), *What is Cultural Studies: A Reader*. London: Arnold, 1997, p. 31.

[14] Archer op cit.

[15] Williams, R. The Long Revolution. London: Verso, 1961/2019.

capitalism and patriarchy, consciousness and self-consciousness are framed by the dominant culture of a particular society. Taking a cue from these, one can analyze aspects of contemporary lived experience such as femaleness and maleness as not simply ways of analyzing the world, but rather modes of social being, and not as essential characteristics of one's ontology.[16] Cultural activism has often been portrayed to be a domain that is best suited for rallying women for the causes of social justice. During the 1980s, a significant section of the progressive cultural organizations adhered to the belief that women are better organized in cultural groups because those groups suit their inherent femaleness that possesses. Two activists have critiqued this attitude in great detail:

> The problem is not that the movement uses women to voice its opinions and stand on issues. That is okay. On the campus as well, we have got these kinds of allegations. People have come up to us and said that we restrict women's mobility within the organizational hierarchy, but the point is that we are working to make them represent themselves. That takes time. Yes, we do accept that some of the groups actually have converted women into instruments for their cultural wings, and that is wrong. (Student Activist, Hyderabad)

> The basic issue about organizing women, Dalits and minorities in mainstream political formations, especially within student politics is that their representation as Rohith Vemula mentioned is often reduced to merely a number. It becomes very difficult to mobilize them because of the casteist, fascist and gendered nature of the society that we live in. In that regard, cultural wings often seem to us like an easy way out because it gives us a safe space to not only talk to them and realize their issues but also to speak about them and hear about

---

[16] Sangari, K. *Politics of the Possible: Essays on Gender, History, Narrative, Colonial English*. New Delhi: Tulika, 1999.

them in their own ways without being overtly political about it. (Student Activist, Bengaluru)

One of the recurring themes that have found space in these narratives from activists is the tendency of their organizations and the movement in general to see women as being mere 'numbers' among their ranks fulfilling the representative purposes of these organizations. In many such cases, women rarely go higher in the organizational hierarchy both within the cultural organization or within the broader organizational set-up that comes to control the cultural organization. Under a socio-political structure, where the question of vanguardism is inextricably linked to the question of culture, culture often plays a key role in how certain communities or groups of people are represented in the political frame of reference.[17]

The uncritical usage of vanguardism as a mode of socio-political mobilization has influenced how socio-political theorization has taken place in South Asia, particularly in India. It has been used as an ideological narrative to counter the evolution of a genuine form of transformative social theory that concerns itself with the true nature of the individual and one's individuality. Most of the social theorizing in India has neglected the importance of subjectivity and the critical role that the individual plays in social transformation, as had been highlighted by Marx.[18] Individuality is composed of both objective and subjective factors produced by an interrelationship of different subjective and objective factors, and the existent social relations in place. The individual is the '"centre of interaction" between individuality ... and the outside world', with the former being specific to a particular human being while the latter being determined by interactions between the human being and the society around the human being in differing spatialities and temporal frameworks[19] The analysis of individuals as subjects requisites the construction of aspects such as space, temporality

---

[17] Hobsbawm, E. *Uncommon People: Resistance, Rebellion and Jazz*. London: Abacus, 1999; Pawar, J. V. *Dalit Panthers: An Authoritative History*. New Delhi: Forward Press, 2017.

[18] Marx, K. *Grundrisse*. London: Penguin, 1993.

[19] Filippini, M. *Using Gramsci: A New Approach*. London: Pluto Press, 2017, p. 25.

and politics as not mere stages upon which antagonisms function but rather as sites of contestation themselves.[20] Students get affected by a range of different factors, the effects of which get further complicated on the campuses because of the inherently complicated nature of the campus space that remains trapped between being a progressive space distinct from the social reality in the broader society and being a part and parcel of the society like any other space. It is this socio-political and cultural position of being entrapped within this contradictory consciousness that makes the cultural activism that occurs within them so important to the analysis of the general state of affairs not only within these spaces but in society as well.

The cultural movement in India, or rather the Indian subcontinent of the pre-1947 days, provided the requisite space for subjectivity within the progressive movement. Jalil's history of the Progressive Writers' Movement shows the diversity of how different reputed members of the PWM defined the idea of progress.[21] Sajjad Zaheer had noted, 'The conception of progress, it was admitted [in the first All India Progressive Writers' Conference], was different for different people; it would change according to place and time'.[22] This subjective belief formed the core ideas surrounding progress that is carried forward by most of the activists in the cultural realm, especially among the students as the following two statements from activists prove:

> The kind of questions that cultural movements present are highly subjective in nature. That is one of the fundamental criticisms that is often accorded to it. But that is important. It is important that we speak about the variety of experiences that a single individual goes through in the process of becoming a true individual. (Cultural Activist, Delhi)

---

[20] Featherstone, D. 'Politicising the Crisis: The Southern Question, Uneven Geographies, and the Construction of Solidarity'. In Ó. G. Agustín, & M. B. Jørgensen (eds.), *Solidarity without Borders*. London: Pluto Press, 2016.

[21] Jalil 2020 op cit.

[22] Zaheer, 1936/2017, op cit.

> I think the basic advantage of cultural resistance is that it allows us to speak about how the same decision affects different people differently. Even in mainstream student politics, it is very difficult for organizations to go into the details and intricacies of every single issue from the perspective of every single student. Because cultural fronts are so much more democratic and freer in nature, they often become extremely important in that regard. (Cultural Activist, Bengaluru)

Cultural resistance offers an alternative to bureaucratic models of socialist imagination that is often celebrated by the middle class and in South Asia, bureaucracy is an important question. It has indeed often resulted in a general upliftment of the marginalized populace, especially through a struggle with feudalism in countries such as India, Pakistan, and Bangladesh.[23] However, the model of upliftment has often been restricted to an economistic understanding of development, one that has failed to generate a sense of participatory democracy among the people and has not been able to generate a sense of subaltern autonomy and has instead resulted in further bureaucratization of the progressive movements and politics.[24] This becomes quite evident if one considers the history of the Communist movement in India.[25] Socio-political theory plays an important role in the process of constructing an uncritical attitude towards the mainstream, which has resulted in some countries of the Global South continuing to remain bound by their traditional and cultural characteristics because of the lack of the necessary structural elements that are required to be incorporated into the

---

[23] Nossiter, T. J. *Marxist State Governments in India*. London: Printer Publishers, 1988.

[24] Nandi, P. 'Communism through the Ballot Box: Over a Quarter Century of Uninterrupted Rule in West Bengal'. Sociological Bulletin, 54(2), 2005, 171-94; Modonesi, M. *Subalternity, Antagonism, Autonomy: Constructing the Political Subject*. London: Pluto Press, 2014.

[25] Nossiter op cit.

global system of modernity.[26] It is important to emphasize that the relationship that exists between structure and agency is one that involves giving rise to specific kinds of practices in society.[27] The complete lack of agency becomes manifest in how bureaucratic administration models sometimes take the economy as the central dominating factor in analyzing society. Berger writes, 'Consciousness may be socially produced, Marxists argue, but it is always filtered through minds of men and women who are active in the world and whose personalities and experiences also shape their conceptions'.[28] Culture is an integral part of how any socio-political ideology desires to shape and alter society. It was none other than Herbert Marcuse, who had written:

> The prevalent material needs and satisfactions are shaped—and controlled—by the requirements of exploitation. Socialism must augment the quantity of good and services in order to abolish all poverty, but at the same time, socialist production must change the quality of existence—change the needs and satisfactions themselves. Moral, psychological, aesthetic, intellectual faculties, which today, if developed at all, are relegated to a realm of culture separate from and above the material existence, would then become factors in the material production itself.[29]

Student protests are a culmination of both the material and ideological contradictions in society, especially when it comes to

---

[26] Desai, A. R. *State and Society in India: Essays in Dissent*. Bombay: Popular Prakashan, 1975; Omvedt, G. '"Modernization" Theories: The Ideology of Empire?'. In A. R. Desai (ed), *Essays on Modernization of Underdeveloped Societies: Volume 1*. New York: Humanities Press, 1972.

[27] Feenberg, A. 'Lukacs's Theory of Reification and Contemporary Social Movements'. Rethinking Marxism, 27(4), 2015, 490-507.

[28] Berger op cit., p. 43.

[29] Marcuse, H. *Counter-Revolution and Revolt*. Seattle: Beacon Press, 1972, p. 3.

voicing the demands of marginalized communities.[30] Cultural resistance plays an important role in this regard. It provides the necessary ideological conditions through which insecurities of the marginalized sections of the populace can be addressed effectively through the creation of a cultural paradigm that makes them feel at one with the space and time within which they find themselves[31] that often allows them to self-identify themselves as being part of a universal struggle against oppression and exploitation—going beyond the context in which their immediate context of exploitation takes place.

---

[30] Whittington, E. L. 'Interracial Dialogue and the Southern Student Human Relations Project'. In R. Cohen & D. J. Snyder (eds), *Rebellion in Black and White: Southern Student Activism in the 1960s*. Baltimore: The John Hopkins University Press, 2013.

[31] Jones, G. S. 'Working-Class Culture and Working-Class Politics in London, 1870-1900: Notes on the Remaking of a Working Class'. Journal of Social History, 7, 1977, 460-508.

Conclusion
Can one Sing to Liberation in 'Unreal' Spaces'?

> A fuller perspective means the view and review of life in its totality which means freedom from the piecemeal and the stereotyped, freedom from the urge to find a formula. [The Point] should be the cultural reconstruction of our country as an indispensable part of our national reconstruction.
>
> Hemanga Biswas[1]

Nationalism has an important connection with the social perceptions surrounding modernity. The majoritarian nationalism, which is currently being propagated as a cultural aspect of Indian nationalism has paved the path for the BJP to push aside the actual economic problems that the nation is facing to the sidelines by replacing it with political jingoism and bourgeois authoritarian nationalism.[2] Post the demolition of the Babri Masjid in 1992, India as a nation has witnessed the rise of the Hindu right-wing as a massive political force.[3] The present situation demands more attention because the extent of the rise of the far-right in India in recent times has surpassed all historical records. The far-right in India has projected its brand of jingoistic nationalism as being the only national culture of India. All national cultures always have two sides—one

---

[1] Biswas, H. 'Hints for a new Manifesto'. In S. Pradhan (ed), *Marxist Cultural Movement in India Volume 2: Chronicles and Documents (1947-1958)*. Kolkata: National Book Agency, 1979.

[2] Menon op cit.

[3] See SAHMAT. *Ayodhya Verdict 2019: Justice Denied*. New Delhi: SAHMAT, 2019.

progressive and one regressive. While one can 'drown in it' as the Bundists did back in Russia and become a bourgeois element oneself, the Leninist position was to transform these struggles into genuinely internationalist ones. Speaking in this regard, Lenin argued that national liberation struggles are particular struggles that take place within a fixed social structure which through the application of revolutionary theory and praxis can be transformed into an internationalist struggle against oppression in general. Lenin stated:

> The elements of democratic and socialist culture are present, if only in rudimentary form, in every national culture, since in every nation there are toiling and exploited masses, whose conditions of life inevitably give rise to the ideology of democracy and socialism. But every nation also possesses a bourgeois culture (and most nations a reactionary and clerical culture as well) in the form, not merely of "elements", but of the dominant culture. Therefore, the general "national culture" is the culture of the landlords, the clergy and the bourgeoisie.[4]

Nationalism in India however is a complex issue and is beyond the scope of this particular book. It is a combination of a fetish with the nation-state (that effectively constituted one of the basic fulcrums of nationalist thought back in the 1970s),[5] as well as a political utilization of culture that goes beyond the nation-state, both geographically and culturally.[6] Modern-day nationalism, in a nutshell, however, 'replaces the "subject" by the "citizen". What constitutes the nation above all is that a 'people' come to believe that they are a distinct people and the factors giving rise to this collective self-belief are immensely varied'—the analysis of which

---

[4] Lenin, V. I. 'Critical Remarks on the National Question.' In *Lenin Collected Works: Volume 20*. Moscow: Progress Publishers, 1913, p. 24.
[5] Debray, R. 'Marxism and the National Question'. *New Left Review*, 1(105), 1977.
[6] Menon op cit.

requires a highly subjective framework.[7] How such a nation reacts to events and ideas is contingent upon the newer forms of culture that are promoted within the country, especially in a country where religious thought has completely coalesced with political ideas and as such has become the political thrust that characterizes a nation.[8] The Indian struggle for freedom had space for both a Pandit Ram Prasad Bismil, a staunch Hindu, who had written lines such as these in chaste Urdu:

> सरफ़रोशी की तमन्ना, अब हमारे दिल में है।
> देखना है ज़ोर कितना, बाज़ु-ए-कातिल में है? ...
> वह जिस्म भी क्या जिस्म है, जिसमें न हो ख़ून-ए-जुनूँ;
> तूफ़ानों से क्या लड़े जो, कश्ती-ए-साहिल में है।[9]

[It is our desire to lay our lives for the Revolution; Now we shall see how much courage the enemy has? ... What body is that body that does not have the spirit of rebellion, How can anybody brave a storm in the sea if the boats are on the shore?][10]

... and an Ashfaqullah Khan, a devout Muslim, who had written in chaste Hindustani:

> है मातृभूमि मैं तेरी सेवा करूंगा
> मुश्किल हज़ार आये ना मैं डरूंगा
> निश्चय यह कर चूका हूँ संदेह कुछ नहीं हैं
> तेरे लिए जीऊंगा तेरे लिए मरूंगा[11]

[O my motherland, I will serve you even if there are a thousand hurdles, I will not be afraid. I have decided this

---

[7] Vanaik, A. *Marxism and Nationalism*. New Delhi: Society for Marxist Studies, 2018, p. 17.

[8] Ibid.

[9] Siddiqui, W. *Do Sarfarosh Shayar: Ashfaqullah and Bismil*. New Delhi: SAHMAT and Raza Foundation, 2018.

[10] Translation by author.

[11] Siddiqui, W. *Do Sarfarosh Shayar: Ashfaqullah and Bismil*. New Delhi: SAHMAT and Raza Foundation, 2018.

and I do not doubt that I will live for you and die for you][12]

The kind of jingoistic nationalism that the BJP has been propagating does not make a distinction between the Indian state and the Indian civilization. They do not have the political sensibility to understand that the Indian struggle for freedom was a struggle for the civilization, i.e., for Indianness, and not only for the land of the nation-state so much so that '... the Indian freedom movement ceased to be an expression of only nationalist consolidation; it came to acquire a new stature as a symbol of the universal struggle for political justice and cultural dignity'.[13] The Indian struggle for freedom was thus quite similar to the international working-class struggle—a universal struggle against oppression because it did not counter merely oppressors but oppression itself, as a concept.

India today, however, is governed by a regime that does not pay heed to this rich legacy of the freedom fighters but rather believes in rampant war-mongering. Under the BJP, Gods, political figures, sports, soldiers, farmers, and even mobile phones have become icons of political hate-mongering. They have been used for harnessing the electoral attention of the crowd and for furthering the agenda of the Hindutva forces.[14] Amidst the conditions created by such a state of affairs, cultural activism is a relatively easier field to find the manifestations of internationalism in India. India benefits from the broad history of cultural exchanges which has characterized its activist realm since the colonial times. Cultural figures from Pakistan and Bangladesh have always played an important role in the cultural student activism landscape in India. Faiz's poems have been important elements of the cultural activism landscape of India, at least in the northern regions and in the central universities. There are two very specific reasons for the same. As a language, Urdu enjoys a certain quality in terms of its phonetics and linguistic

---

[12] Translation by author.

[13] Nandy, A. *The Illegitimacy of Nationalism: Rabindranath Tagore and the Politics of Self*. Delhi: Oxford University Press, 1994.

[14] Deb Roy, S. *Mass Struggles and Leninism*. New Delhi: Phoneme, 2022.

beauty, which often makes it a preferable language of emotional expression, especially those emotions that could often not be expressed in a language suitable for lyrical expositions in other languages.[15] Secondly, the popularity of Urdu has also been accelerated by the kind of influence that Bollywood or the Hindi Film Industry has had in the country. The kind of Hindi that is most commonly used in Hindi films, is an admixture of Hindustani and Urdu, and these films occupy around 43% of the net revenue of the entire film industry in India.[16] Hence, despite a significant number of Indian people not being professionally or socially trained in Urdu have developed a sense of certain words and phrases and their usage in Urdu. This cannot be considered to be unnatural since the genesis of Urdu as a language was in India.[17]

The BJP's war cry against the language is an act of treason against the very cultural framework that guides the Indian civilization. This is especially critical for progressive politics because contemporary progressive politics has been confronted with a wide array of challenges, both from the right wing of the political spectrum and from the left wing. While the former has been launching a frontal attack on the freedom of expression, the latter has also been plagued by the growing tensions surrounding sectarianism, revisionism and bureaucratism, which have only increased in recent times.

Under the aegis of contemporary capitalism, it is thus critical 'to distinguish between the need for changing intolerable conditions of existence and the need for changing the society as a

---

[15] A Cultural Activist from Delhi, Personal Communication, 2022.

[16] See https://web.archive.org/web/20160114100635/http://www2.deloitte.com/content/dam/Deloitte/in/Documents/technology-media-telecommunications/in-tmt-economic-contribution-of-motion-picture-and-television-industry-noexp.pdf [Accessed 25.07.2023]

[17] University College London. Urdu Language: History and Development. Available at: https://www.ucl.ac.uk/atlas/urdu/language.html#:~:text=Urdu%20started%20developing%20in%20north,Persian%2C%20as%20well%20as%20Turkish [Accessed 25.07.2023]

whole'.[18] The former can be achieved within the aegis of an established society quantitatively, while for the latter, one needs a qualitative change[19] that requires a critique of the objectivity form of the capitalist society that often results in an objectification of subjective experiences, both objectively and subjectively.[20] Social transformation requires both ideology and an analysis of material transformation that comes from historical analysis with one complementing the other rather than one dominating the other.[21] This intersection of ideology and material oppression becomes extremely important in the context of India where numerous identities based on one's social attributes become extremely important in the production of the socio-cultural fabric.

Identity politics is an important aspect of campus politics in contemporary India. It has been an important facet of the students' movement and will, in all possibilities and probabilities, remain so in the near future. This is quite evident in the ways in which the anti-caste movements have affected the broad contours of student politics in general in the country both infusing it with the spirit of a critical attitude towards social justice that goes beyond class reductionism as well as making it vulnerable to the influences of liberal postmodernism.[22]

The importance that cultural resistance holds within the students' movement is immense. It not only provides the movement with a certain vibrancy but also allows the movement to stay connected to the world beyond the campus. Campuses, especially the residential ones, in India, are designed in a manner in which they can act as islands of excellence—existing outside the contours of society free from the contradictions that dictate

---

[18] Marcuse, H. 'Liberation from the Affluent Society'. In D. Kellner (ed.), *Collected Papers of Herbert Marcuse: Volume 3*. London: Routledge, 1967/2005.

[19] ibid.

[20] Pitkin, H. F. 'Rethinking Reification'. *Theory and Society*, *16*(2), 1987, 263–293.

[21] Shah, A. '"The muck of the past": revolution, social transformation, and the Maoists in India'. *Journal of the Royal Anthropological Institute, 20*(2), 2014, 337–356.

[22] PS, S., & Sawant, P. B. (2018). *Mandal Commission: Rashtra Nirman ki Sabse Badi Pahal*. New Delhi: Leftword Books and Free Media; Singh et al. 2022 op cit.

the social existence of the majority of the people. Universities in India are thus, as an old trade unionist commented, unreal spaces. India, as it stands, is a society that has been in a state where it has had to launch a constant struggle against the forces of feudal traditionalism and modern neoliberal capitalism simultaneously. Neoliberal capitalism has been constantly launching a frontal attack on the 'public' nature of university spaces, not only in India but also globally transforming these spaces into highly commoditized spaces, discouraging the flow of critical thought, and generating a one-dimensional acceptance of the state of affairs.[23]

The constant effect of neoliberalism on such spaces has resulted in the complete marginalization of students coming from weaker socio-economic and cultural backgrounds, one that is only going to increase with the institutionalization of the New Education Policy of the BJP Government.[24] Cultural protest and its associated forms of art disrupt the dominantly commodified relationship between art and commerce. It plays an important role in devising the methods through which the complicated narratives surrounding society and capital can be transformed into a popular logic easily accessible to the people. The Indian People's Theatre Association was formed during turbulent times which represented the importance of this very ability of the cultural modes of protest and rebellion.[25] Mihir Bhattacharya writes:

> The people, both rural and urban, were ready for the new politics of culture in the era of movements and struggles; the elite and the modernist had to respond to their needs and desires and talk their language before the people would join. That is why

---

[23] Callinicos, A. *Universities in a Neoliberal World*. London: Bookmarks, 2006.

[24] Chakraborty, S., & Ambedkar, P. (eds.) Students Won't be Quiet. New Delhi: Leftword, 2022; Narayanan, N., & Dhar, D. (eds.). *Education or Exclusion? The Plight of Indian Students*. New Delhi: Leftword, 2022.

[25] Singh, M. M. P. 'National Context of Progressive Movement'. In *The Progressive Cultural Movement: A Critical History*. New Delhi: SAHMAT, 2017; Chuhan, C. 'Progressive Literary Movement in Hindi-Urdu Region'. In *The Progressive Cultural Movement: A Critical History*. New Delhi: SAHMAT, 2017.

the new consciousness of the avant-garde, shaped by aspirations for political, intellectual and cultural modernity, sought to express itself particularly in music, dance, drama and cinema, all of which could be accessed easily by the people, and most which could spread messages by word of mouth at incredible speed. This is the reason why the Left-wing movement in culture, which started in the 1930s and spread to all parts of India in no time, took up the performing arts in a big way.[26]

Under capitalism, such cultural exchanges become commodified. Economic exchanges, often form the foundation of these relations and vice versa. Culture under contemporary capitalism is a commodity that can be utilized for various purposes. Cultural practices reflect the organic lifestyles of the community to which they belong. However, these practices do not exist in isolation and are a part and parcel of the social mode of production in totality which dominates the society beyond the boundaries of the ethnic group's individual existence. These practices modify and get modified by their relationships with other cultures which often alter their pristinely unique traditional characteristics. In the context of North-East India, the most famous cultural practices revolve around the songs and dance forms of the indigenous populace emphasizing the vibrantly picturesque landscapes of their region along with their agricultural practices. Be it Assam's Bihu, or Manipur's Jagoi or Mizoram's Cheraw, indigenous cultural expressions have traditionally located themselves outside the realm of capitalist commodity production and have been intimately connected with modes of sustenance economy based on the domination of use value rather than price or exchange values.[27] With the development of capitalism, the use value of objects is rendered

---

[26] Bhattacharya, M. (2017). Moment and Movement: Creativity in the Cause of the People. In *The Progressive Cultural Movement: A Critical History*. New Delhi: SAHMAT, 2017, p. 47.

[27] Deb Roy, S. 'Ethnic Cultural Expressions of the North-East: Ecofeminism and Enrichment Capitalism'. In S. Phukan (ed), *Trends in Contemporary Language, Literature and Culture*. Guwahati: Purbayan, 2021.

obsolete and there occurs the complete domination of the exchange value resulting in the creation of commodities,[28] which dominate contemporary society.

The importance of cultural struggles in such a situation is immense considering that cultural struggles are quite intimately related to how one determines the relationship that exists between the base and superstructure under capitalism, which again inadvertently turns into a debate between the economic structure and the political and cultural structure of the society. Contemporary capitalism needs to be thought of as a system in itself rather than simply an economic structure.[29] And there is no way one can make a sense of the society under such a social system by leaving out culture from the milieu. Culture and its associated modes of expression are parts of the overall ways in which the social means of production seek to control, dominate, and exploit the people, especially those that come from the marginalized sections of the population. As Karl Marx had noted in 1859:

> In the social production of their existence, men inevitably enter into definite relations, which are independent of their will, namely relations of production appropriate to a given stage in the development of their material forces of production. The totality of these relations of production constitutes the economic structure of society, the real foundation, on which arises a legal and political superstructure and to which correspond definite forms of social consciousness. The mode of production of material life conditions the general process of social, political and intellectual life. It is not the consciousness of men that determines their existence, but their social existence that determines their consciousness.[30]

---

[28] Marx, K. Capital: Volume 1. London: Penguin, 1976.

[29] Fraser, N. 'Contradictions of Capital and Care'. *New Left Review*, 100, 2016, 99-117

[30] Marx, K. 'A Contribution to the Critique of Political Economy', in Marx Engels Collected Works: Volume 29. London: Lawrence and Wishart, 1859/1987, p. 263.

South Asia because of its unique geopolitical and social nature has been an important, yet unexplored, domain of mainstream social theoretical traditions. The journey that South Asia, and especially India, has traversed as a region has often been conceptualized as a highly heterodox one where both tradition and modernity have played a crucial role. Countries such as India have failed to replicate the success of the colonial model of administration as found in Europe because European settlers attempted to replicate a relatively egalitarian (capitalist) model through local structures of authority based on pre-capitalist inequalities,[31] many of which continue to exert a tremendous influence on the marginalized populace.[32] The mainstream ideas surrounding social progress and modernity in India as many argue continue to be dictated by the paradigm of colonialism.[33] But most of them agree that the contemporary state of India manifests the contradiction between tradition and modernity, where even organizations such as the Communist Parties have often had to take recourse to religious sentiments to attract people.[34] The tradition of egalitarian social thought in India has had to pass through many hurdles, one of which was the absence of a proper revolutionary tradition in India that had always distinguished it from other countries in Asia such as China and Vietnam.[35] Because of its unique socio-political and historical inheritance, the Indian society despite not being an underdeveloped society as far as social organization and social structure is considered 'which [had] remained at a stage of

---

[31] Weiner, M. 'Political Problems of Modernizing Pre-Industrial Societies'. In A. R. Desai (ed), *Essays on Modernization of Underdeveloped Societies: Volume 1*. New York: Humanities Press, 1972.

[32] Harriss-White 2010 op cit.

[33] Omvedt op cit.

[34] Philip, B. 'In India, Kerala's leaders mix tropical communism with religion to appeal to the Hindu electorate'. Le Monde, 2023, January 03. Available at: https://www.lemonde.fr/en/international/article/2023/01/03/in-india-kerala-s-leaders-mix-tropical-communism-with-religion-to-appeal-to-the-hindu-electorate_6010200_4.html [Accessed 25.07.2023]

[35] Sen Gupta, B. *Communism in Indian Politics*. New Delhi: Young Asia Publications, 1978.

technological and scientific progress roughly comparable to the Renaissance in Europe', it has continued to be dominated by pre-capitalist forms of exploitation.[36] It is in this context that one needs to analyze the state of the progressive cultural movement among students. The history of cultural resistance in India is an old one, and according to some of the activists, goes well beyond the contours of recorded history, such that even a bloody partition and widespread state repression could not do away with it and it has instead increased in recent times.[37]

Cultural activism, like cultural studies, is primarily associated with the generation and analysis of alternative meanings[38] from a perspective inspired by social change. Theories such as dogmatic Marxism continue 'to belie the hope it had initially held out on that score. The promise that such a move would eventually steer Marxism out of its purported ontological crisis -which is essentially the outcome of the reduction of a critical science to a doctrinaire 'communistology'—is on the verge of a miscarriage. That is certainly the case, at least, in sub-continental South Asia. Unsurprisingly, therefore, "culturally-turned" Marxism survives as the sign of the very crisis it was meant to surpass'.[39]

Cultural Marxism in its truest sense would fulfill the role of the critical relationship that needs to exist between local circumstances and the global movement for social justice, emancipation, and liberation. Cultural modes of protest most effectively mediate the dialectics of the local and the global. Cultural struggle has the ability to use conventional local symbols in a much more effective manner than economic and

---

[36] Karve, I. 'Caste and Modernization'. In A. R. Desai (ed), *Essays on Modernization of Underdeveloped Societies: Volume 1*. New York: Humanities Press, 1972.

[37] Hossain, A. 'Cultural Movement in East Pakistan'. In S. Pradhan (ed), *Marxist Cultural Movement in India: Chronicles and Documents (1943-1964): Volume 3*. Kolkata: National Book Agency, 1952/2017; Sharma, R. B. 'The New Culture of the Telugu People'. In S. Pradhan (ed), *Marxist Cultural Movement in India: Chronicles and Documents (1943-1964): Volume 3*. Kolkata: National Book Agency, 1952/2017.

[38] Spillman, L. 'Culture as Meaning Making'. In *Cultural Sociology*, London: Blackwell, 2002.

[39] Ghosh, P. *Insurgent Metaphors: Essays in Culture and Class*. New Delhi: Aakar Books, 2010, p. 13.

purely political ones.[40] At the same time, it has the ability to do that while being conversant with global political tendencies. The importance of local events and contextual issues in the cultural movement in India has always been critical and the ways in which it has reacted the same to global issues has received considerable attention from the masses. Since 2014, the idea of a cultural struggle has become more pertinent, especially because of the ways in which the Bhartiya Janata Party (BJP) government has infiltrated the domains of ideology and hegemony in the everyday lives of the citizens of India. The constant hounding of progressive intellectuals, students and activists has created a stir among the critical citizens of the country. A ruling class that thrives on the generation and propagation of hatred fears a radical and progressive cultural movement because it has the ability to mitigate the problems caused by enmity between the ruling classes, which often trickles down right to the bottom of the social hierarchy making enemies out of people who ideally should have been friends.[41] Progressive cultural activism has the ability to use the notion of happiness in a manner that transcends literature from merely being a cultural entity to a social one.[42] In fact, it is the ability of the cultural movement to engage with the emotional condition of the masses invoking feelings of happiness, anger, and sadness among them by exploring the nuanced everyday life that they lead thus affecting the dominant political culture in the society[43] that makes it a vital force within a democracy. The radical possibilities of human imaginings in terms of weaving a story, a play or a ballad are best captured in the following lines by Antonio Negri:

---

[40] See for example the growth of IPTA in different parts of India: Roy, A. 'Singing their way towards a better world: People's Songs Movement in Late Colonial and Early-Independence Bengal'. In *The Progressive Cultural Movement: A Critical History*. New Delhi: SAHMAT, 2017; Dewri, P. 'IPTA and the Music of Assam'. In *The Progressive Cultural Movement: A Critical History*. New Delhi: SAHMAT, 2017.

[41] Haqqani, H. *India vs Pakistan: Kashmir. Terrorism. N-Bomb: Why Can't we Just be Friends?* New Delhi: Juggernaut, 2016.

[42] Premchand op cit.

[43] Biswas 1979 op cit.; Berger op cit.

> We are obliged to construct, through the abstract and with abstract materials, a new reality, a new movement. But a movement is the telling of a story. The future event is constructed by a storytelling. The crisis of the revolutionary event is tied to the failure of revolutionary storytelling, and only a new storytelling will succeed in determining, let's not say a revolutionary event, but even its thinkability.[44]

The generation of imagination was a critical part of how groups such as the IPTA, the JANAM, and others like that have functioned over the years. They had to undergo numerous hurdles in staging a performance such as creating makeshift stages, constructing plays quickly, making changes at the last moment, etc.[45] The progressive cultural movement among the students also has to undergo similar issues, as one of the activists recounts, 'The kind of performances we put up come after a lot of hard work. We have to undergo a lot of issues, loss of stages, lack of proper funding to put up a play, etc. All of these come at a cost. The very fact that we are continuing to do this work is itself revolutionary' (Cultural Activist, Delhi). Despite the difficulties, the activists continue to do the work because they realize that the cultural struggle is an inevitable part of the broader movement. The analysis of cultural resistance brings one to analyze how everyday lives influence the performativity associated with the cultural experience of a particular group or individual,[46] and vice versa. It is important to understand that humans do not dance before meat—a maxim that thought never forgets. So that it may know how to return to the thing that is needful, and not soar too high. Like that of the beasts, mankind's hunger is seldom one-storied; the more men eat, the more they hunger'.[47] It is this cycle of the desire to accumulate that drives human beings under capitalism. This has become extremely complicated with 'the rise

---

[44] Negri, A. *Art and Multitude*. Trans. Ed Emery. London: Polity, 2011, pp. 73-74.

[45] Ghosh 2012 op cit.

[46] Diawara op cit.

[47] Bloch, E. *A Philosophy of the Future*. Trans. J. Cumming. New York: Herder and Herder, 1970, p. 4.

to hegemony of a new kind of international finance capital ... based on a process of globalization of finance'[48] because it has caused an eradication of the human nature of the everyday life of the people causing widescale poverty and hopelessness to arise in their lives. In the context of India, this has been accompanied by a form of neo-fascist regime that has promoted a kind of what Anand Teltumbde calls Neoliberal Hindutva that feeds on both economic and cultural exploitation.[49] It has resulted in the creation of a society, where Islam and everything connected with it has been deemed to be an enemy of the Indian State and the people therein with the people of Pakistan being publicly demonstrated as lower human beings,[50] much like how historically African people have been often used as 'a synonym for the non-human or lesser human being that justified enslavement, slavery, colonialism and exploitation'.[51]

The 'health of the state of [culture is] a mark of the state of [the] civilization and democracy'.[52] The progressive cultural movement among the students is critical because they have been able to invoke the contemporary relevance of poets such as Vilas Ghogre, Gorakh Pandey and Pash, who otherwise have been completely relegated by the forces of neoliberal capitalism. The cultural movement is a part of the broader political movement, like the students' movement. And in bringing into effect the change that it so desires, the movement will need the dark humor

---

[48] Patnaik, P. 'The Accumulation Process in the Period of Globalisation'. Economic and Political Weekly, 43(26-27), 2008, p. 109. Available at: https://www.epw.in/journal/2008/26-27/perspectives/accumulation-process-period-globalisation.html [Accessed 25.07.2023]

[49] Teltumbde, 2018 op cit.

[50] See https://m.economictimes.com/news/politics-and-nation/sitaram-yechury-warns-against-moving-towards-a-hindu-pakistan/articleshow/59991592.cms [Accessed 25.07.2023]

[51] Manji, F. 'Amílcar Cabral and the Politics of Culture and Identity'. *Logos: A Journal of Modern Society and Culture*, 2023. Available at: https://logosjournal.com/2023/amilcar-cabral-and-the-politics-of-culture-and-identity/ [Accessed 10.08.2023]

[52] Menon op cit., p. 6.

of Saadat Hasan Manto[53] as well as the clarity of Hemanga Biswas. It will require the internationalism that has bridged continents of working classes against oppression and the secular patriotism of the Indian working class which resisted fascism and exploitation in their own particular social contexts.[54] The cause of the revolution shares an intrinsic connection with knowledge, and as such with how knowledge is implemented in the everyday life of the people. The cultural mode of expressing dissent allows one to voice one's opinion in one's own language regardless of how one is situated within the state of being in society. In the Universities, the cultural movement of the students is an extremely important part of keeping alive the tradition of dissent in India. Because campuses are designed in such a way that they represent the most progressive ideals of society—both physically and ideologically—it often becomes quite easy for students and their movements to fall into the trap of abject utopianism obsessing over the arguments that they want to make that often gets directed by the space that they occupy—a space that is often at odds with the broader society.

This is where Marx became so important, especially how he differed from the utopian socialists. Marx never distanced himself from the actual struggles of the working class, in contrast with the other utopian socialists who preached mere reorganization but not a radical reconstruction of the foundations of the society[55]. The students' movement can learn a significant much from this distinction because it often remains constrained to the issues of the campus or the contradictions that it faces as students. They can gain critically from being more

---

[53] The dark humour gets aptly manifested in statements such as *'The war has made graves also more expensive'*. See Manto, S. H. 'Progressive Graveyards'. In H. Narang (Trans. And Ed), *Manto My Love*. New Delhi: Sahitya Akademi, 2018, p. 167.

[54] Ahmad, A. 'The Progressive Movement in its International Setting'. In *The Progressive Cultural Movement: A Critical History*. New Delhi: SAHMAT, 2017; Awasthi, R. 'Historical Perspective of Progressive Literary Movement'. In *The Progressive Cultural Movement: A Critical History*. New Delhi: SAHMAT, 2017

[55] Dunayevskaya, R. 'Marx and the Utopian Socialists'. In *The Raya Dunayevskaya Collection—Marxist-Humanism: A Half Century of its World Development*. Detroit: Wayne State University Archives of Labor and Urban Affairs, 1956.

connected to the wider struggles ensuing in society, something that has been the case quite evidently with the recent student struggles in the country. However, there is a long way to go, specifically because the overall composition of the student movement itself has undergone quite a radical shift in recent years, especially with the effects of the neoliberal reforms creeping up within the general composition of the student populace on the campuses that have made the campuses akin to an 'elite' space much like the rest of the mainstream society. The cultural movement because of its very nature of being rooted in the everyday contradictions of the common masses, can make the students' movement connect to the everyday life of people. It can thus also make such spaces sing the ballad of liberation.

Afterword
Yes, to our Songs of Liberation! Yes, to Freedom!

THE SONGS OF OUR FOREBEARERS AND DREAMING BEYOND DESPAIR AND DISILLUSIONMENT

Ndindi Kitonga[1]

> I came here for revolution, not just to perform.
> —Hemanga Biswas

> Becoming radical isn't an impulsive dalliance. It's a leap toward allowing yourself to believe in the possibility of collective survival—and to believe that even if we don't make it, we are still worth fighting for, to the last breath. —Maya Schenwar[2]

THE SONGS OF OUR FOREBEARERS

I am incredibly humbled to write this afterward. I am a diasporic East African living and working in the United States, struggling against empire from within. Most of the scholarship and organizing I do is in the realm of Black feminism, abolition, anti-colonial movements, internationalism, and democratic education.

---

[1] Kenyan-American Revolutionary Educator and Organiser, Los Angeles, Co-Founder Palms Unhoused Mutual Aid (PUMA), Los Angeles
[2] Maya Schenwar, foreword to Let This Radicalize You by Hayes, Kelly, and Mariame Kaba. (2023). Chicago: Haymarket Books.

Being asked to provide an afterword for a book that provides so much insight and joy that taps into an important aspect yet oft-discarded aspect of movement work is such an honor.

While studying the machinations of capitalist domination and all antagonisms must be an important component of movement work, we can not forget that people already understand themselves as being exploited and alienated. The young people presented in this book are making material demands with their expressions. They indeed have an analysis of the issues surrounding sexism, ethnicism, fascism, and poverty. They also want to embrace their full humanity and meet their immaterial (some might even say spiritual) needs. They demand bread, roses, and song!

Resistance through and with political theatre, art-making, song, and all other humanizing cultural expressions have always been an important part of the struggle. This is not just a way to express deep anger, reclaim colonized identities, or even self-soothe. Cultural resistance practices are ideological and philosophical interventions. They provide community-building opportunities and spaces to articulate ideas and challenge status-quo understandings of issues while allowing for new art forms and tactics for movements to emerge. We've always needed artists, truth-tellers, political theatre, dance, and many forms of expression to complement and drive political social political change.

This book is not only descriptive of current movements. Indeed it is a study of the work of the forebearers, ancestors, and elders who inform the student activism Roy is exploring. I for one was enlivened learning about the political yearnings of Faiz, the clarity of Biswas, the defiance of Habib, and the revolutionary passion of Hashmi. Their words and work remain alive bringing forward piercing truths, sharp condemnations of oppressive structures, and prophetic longings for a liberatory future.

Student movement-makers are not only learning from their revolutionary ancestors, but they are also building upon the work of organizations like the Indian Progressive Theatre Association (IPTA) and the Progressive Writers' Association (PWA) which have a long history of this work. These important organizations and others offer a pathway to a cultural mode of activism and a passageway to display mass refusal. What struck me was how students are not merely regurgitating performances of the past but making their own relevant and contextual art through their work in these organizations as leaders, writers, actors, and lyricists. They are adopting creative campus actions that keep themselves safe while claiming public space for public discourse. Student activists are also finding ingenious ways of sustaining indigenous practices, questioning modernity and eurocentric ways of being. Their embrace of indigeneity and culture is in contrast to jingoistic expressions of identity and tradition their political climate imposes on them.

    I was also heartened to find instances of internationalism fueling the student movement work. Student activists are having discussions about intersectionality and international solidarity building around issues like #metoo, where heterosexism and gendered violence are being examined as systems of domination that must be confronted on multiple fronts, all while maintaining clarity about what to do on the local level. Students are also running on the spark ignited by the 2020 George Floyd Rebellion and Global Black Lives Matter Movement and taking on issues of police brutality and state repression on their campuses.

    Hemanga Biswas decades-old folk song about the shared struggles of Black revolutionary Paul Robeson and India's working and minoritized classes is another beautiful example of this expression of solidarity, the students are drawing from.

> [They don't allow us to raise our voice; My negro brother Paul Robeson; We sing in our raised voice. They don't like, they don't like, My negro brother Paul Robeson; They're fear-struck Robeson, They're fear-struck as they hear our war cry, They're fear-struck as they see our red eye, They're fear-struck as they feel our bravery, Robeson, My negro brother Paul Robeson; They are afraid of living, They are afraid of the dead, They are afraid of remembering, They are afraid of those dreams; They are afraid Robeson. They are afraid of the

> People's Movement, They are afraid of our Unity,
> They are afraid of our Courage, They are afraid of
> their own demise]

As I read through the text, making sense of how student movements are allowing for cultural expressions to inform social identity formation along with political organizing, I'm reminded of the work of Cabral on culture.

> Whatever may be the ideological or idealistic characteristics of cultural expression, culture is an essential element of the history of a people. Culture is, perhaps, the product of this history just as the flower is the product of a plant. Like history, or because it is history, culture has as its material base the level of the productive forces and the mode of production. Culture plunges its roots into the physical reality of the environmental humus in which it develops, and it reflects the organic nature of the society, which may be more or less influenced by external factors. History allows us to know the nature and extent of the imbalances and conflicts (economic, political, and social) which characterize the evolution of a society; culture allows us to know the dynamic synthesis which have been developed and established by social conscience to resolve these conflicts at each stage of its evolution, in the search for survival and progress.

Cultural resistance and practices allow us to understand where we are in our struggles, what phase we are in, the level of people's commitment, and emergent contradictions. All movements bear contradictions. The young organizers discussed here are careful not to culturally appropriate or speak over the work of ethnic and gendered minorities but the state repression and economic pressures some are facing don't allow for the full participation of all. While students are working toward more democratic forms of organizing the art, they need to find ways to keep going, support their most vulnerable members, and challenge the authoritarian state. That is no small task. To address these contradictions, the student campus movements must also continue to maintain a dialectical relationship between local-level praxis and international liberation-making. Even with these challenges, it's vital we support and celebrate the student organizers' experiment with the possibilities of democratic non-chauvinistic participation in a future society......the liberatory future their forebearers wept, wrote, and sang for.

DREAMING BEYOND DESPAIR AND DISILLUSIONMENT

Dreams occur while one is at rest, and they only come when we're not moving in relation to capitalist time, also says a lot about the futures they could enact. To dream of freedom is to take seriously the act of stopping to think pausing to consider- hesitating. The dream occurs in the break. Though there is no inherent righteousness to dreams to those for whom this real-world reality cannot be accepted, a different kind of reality not yet discovered is a beautiful thing.—Josh Myers[3]

This book is a reminder that we need to turn towards each other in revolutionary siblinghood. It is a call to revive a rich tradition of cultural activism across India and a celebration of emergent critical vibrant grassroots, people-centered student movements. Very importantly, this is also a book in the art of revolutionary dreaming, of embracing new possibilities. This is not a utopian type of dreaming or hoping but a practice in real-time everyday art-making communities have engaged in overtime in their liberatory pursuits. As Kelly Hayes notes, "The struggle for freedom and transformation is not a dream. It's a fire burning in real-time. And the blaze is spreading."[4]

These songs of liberation are being sung in concert with, and as projects that critique empire, and denounce Hindu nationalism and the rise of neo-fascism, all while enduring

---

[3] Myers, Joshua (2023). On Black Study. (pp.184). Chicago: Pluto Press

[4] Hayes, Kelly (2014), On the Cusp of Change https://transformativespaces.org/2014/12/18/on-the-cusp-of-change/

repression from within the academy, and agitating against an authoritarian state that understands itself as "the largest democracy in the world".

The book is also a triumph in cultural resistance as a means of connecting local student struggles and movements outside of their immediate context. Deb Roy offers a materialist analysis throughout the text weaving poetry, prose, and activists' direct thoughts connecting them to the structural issues they aim to address. As vital and as vibrant as the movements shared here are, there's a call for deeper engagement with sectors outside of universities, further theorizing and mobilization, so even more join in these songs of freedom.

I end by reminding the reader of the words of internationalist, anti-colonial philosopher, Franz Fanon who declares in his introduction to Black Skin, White Masks that "Human is a yes that vibrates to cosmic harmonies." Later on, at the end of the book, he writes,

> I said in my introduction that human is a yes. I will never stop reiterating that. Yes to life. Yes to love. Yes to generosity. But human is also a no. No to scorn of humans. No to degradation of humans. No the exploitation of humans. No to the butchery of what is most human: freedom.[5]

We hope all who engage with this book are reminded of the revolutionary fire that propelled our ancestors, that warmed the soul-minds of our tired freedom fighters, sustained our mothers, and blazed passionately through the student revolutionaries of our day. Yes to vibrating to our cosmic harmonies in solidarity! Yes to our songs of liberation! Yes to Freedom!

---

[5] Fanon, Frantz [1952]1986. Black Skin, White Masks. (pp. 5). London: Pluto Press. Note: I changed the word "man" to "human" for a more gender-inclusive interpretation.

Printed in the USA
CPSIA information can be obtained
at www.ICGtesting.com
LVHW020543040924
789995LV00003B/611